Fifty Great
WAR FILMS

OSPREY
PUBLISHING

Fifty
Great
WAR
FILMS

TIM NEWARK

First published in Great Britain in 2016 by Osprey Publishing,
PO Box 883, Oxford, OX1 9PL, UK
1385 Broadway, 5th Floor, New York, NY 10018, USA
E-mail: info@ospreypublishing.com

OSPREY PUBLISHING, PART OF BLOOMSBURY PUBLISHING PLC

A CIP catalogue record for this book is available from the British Library

Tim Newark has asserted his right under the Copyright, Designs and Patents Act, 1988, to be identified as
the Author of this Work.

ISBN: 978 1 47282 000 6
PDF ISBN: 978 1 47282 001 3
ePub ISBN: 978 1 47282 002 0

Typeset in Gill Sans and Bellamie
Originated by PDQ Media, Bungay, UK
Printed in Slovenia by GPS Group

15 16 17 18 19 10 9 8 7 6 5 4 3 2 1

All images are from The Kobal Collection

Osprey Publishing supports the Woodland Trust, the UK's leading woodland conservation charity. Between
2014 and 2018 our donations will be spent on their Centenary Woods project in the UK.

www.ospreypublishing.com

INTRODUCTION

In past centuries, great battles and the sacrifice of soldiers were often commemorated by large statues erected in capital cities. The Parthenon frieze on the Acropolis in Athens portrays the ancient Greek warriors who defeated the Persians and kept their civilisation free. In the heart of London, the statue of Nelson raised high on a column celebrates his victory at the battle of Trafalgar over Napoleon – the man who wanted to conquer all of Europe. Today, alongside days of remembrance and the erection of new memorials, we most frequently and widely commemorate our battles and soldiers through war movies.

Ever since the beginning of the 20th century, filmed dramas have been the major way we understand and appreciate past conflicts. As befits a free society, these films are often critical of the conduct of past battles and question the value of so much loss, but they also present the individual courage, camaraderie and professionalism of soldiers. From the very first war documentary depicting the battle of the Somme, to perennial film favourites, such as *Battle of Britain* and *The Longest Day*, they remain the most popular art form that reminds us of the duty and sacrifice of our armed forces. These are the war memorials of today.

Tim Newark, 2016

CONTENTS

18. The Great Escape (1963)
19. 633 Squadron (1964)
20. Von Ryan's Express (1965)
21. The Dirty Dozen (1967)
22. Where Eagles Dare (1968)
23. Hell in the Pacific (1969)
24. Battle of Britain (1969)
25. Oh! What a Lovely War (1969)
26. M*A*S*H (1970)
27. Patton (1970)
28. Tora! Tora! Tora! (1970)
29. A Bridge Too Far (1977)
30. Cross of Iron (1977)
31. The Deer Hunter (1978)
32. Apocalypse Now (1979)
33. The Big Red One (1980)
34. Gallipoli (1981)
35. Das Boot (1981)
36. Come and See (1985)
37. Platoon (1986)
38. Schindler's List (1993)
39. The Thin Red Line (1998)
40. Saving Private Ryan (1998)
41. Three Kings (1999)
42. Behind Enemy Lines (2001)
43. Black Hawk Down (2001)
44. Enemy at the Gates (2001)
45. Downfall (2004)
46. Flags of Our Fathers (2006)
47. The Hurt Locker (2008)
48. Inglourious Basterds (2009)
49. Fury (2014)
50. American Sniper (2014)

THE BATTLE OF THE SOMME

Date: **1916**   Duration: **74 min**

Director:

Geoffrey H Malins

A poster for *The Battle of the Somme*. The film was a great success, both in the UK and abroad, being shown in numerous cinemas for months after its initial release.

A documentary about combat on the Western Front in World War I, *The Battle of the Somme* was released as a feature film and proved enormously popular, attracting some 20 million cinemagoers in its first six weeks. It is often called a propaganda film, but it does little to glamorise the fighting and shows the dead and wounded on both sides in a remarkably humane depiction of the war.

The film begins with preparations for the great Allied offensive on the Somme in June 1916; we are shown the vast number of horses needed to transport armies and striking images of massive piles of shell cases. We see the ferocious artillery onslaught on the German positions, including 'plum pudding' bombs for smashing barbed wire. The cinematographers know that the audience – made up of many parents and families of the serving soldiers – are as interested in the everyday lives of their men on the front line as the fighting, and they show the soldiers having dinner in camp the night before the attack, cooking food in a big pot, and fixing wire cutters on to their rifles.

The battle itself begins with the iconic image of a massive mine ignited on Hawthorn Ridge, sending up a great plume of earth. We then see soldiers going 'over the top' from their trench, but this scene was a later recreation shot behind the lines and is one of the few false moments in the documentary. It does, however, have a feature film sensibility as we then see

Special Attraction throughout the Week ! !

...nday, Tuesday, and Wednesday, October 9, 10, 11—

...r Six Days, with MATINEE every Afternoon at 2.30,

...reat Battle of the Somme,

...VE PARTS. Official Pictures of the British Army in France, taken by permission of the War Office.

This Film will be shown about 2.30, 6.30, and 8 30 p.m.

...HTING the GERMAN AIR RAIDERS. Another startling picture.

...REED—14th Episode in 2 Parts. Pathe's Animated Gazette.

...sday, Friday, and Saturday, October 12, 13, 14—

GREAT BATTLE of the SOMME, in 5 Parts.

...ROES OF THE DARDANELLES, in Two Parts,

...g the GREAT LANDING AT GALLIPOLI. A fine patriotic Drama that will reach the hearts of all.

...nes in and around the British Headquarters. Official War Film.

PATHE'S GAZETTE.

...Seats may be booked in advance for any Evening during the week for the 6.30 p.m. shows. After each Performance, the Hall will be cleared to avoid over...

Commence at 2.30, 6 0, and 8 30 o'clock.

...rices: 1s., 7d., and 4d., including Government Tax.

This scene, showing British troops advancing into no man's land, was actually filmed at the British Third Army mortar school near St Pol, France, and was one of the few staged for the film.

these soldiers disappear into the mist of no man's land. Harsh reality is provided by scenes of a wounded soldier being carried back to his trench, who we are told then died shortly after filming. Towards the end of the film, we are shown the dead and wounded of both sides. We see streams of German prisoners of war, shell shattered trenches, and a dead dog that went in with his master during the attack. The bizarre landscape created by war is depicted by men scrambling up the sides of a 40-foot-deep shell crater.

The film ends on a positive note with cheery soldiers waving to folks at home and a map showing 12 miles of captured territory. But the undeniable reality of the film must have been shocking for some on the home-front and undoubtedly contributed to its popularity – it was shown in numerous cinemas in the UK and abroad for months afterwards – as it expressed so much more than newspaper reports could. *The Battle of the Somme* can truly be seen as the first great war film.

The destructive power of modern artillery was revealed to audiences in this scene of intense barrages prior to the Somme Offensive.

ALL QUIET ON THE WESTERN FRONT

Date: **1930** Duration: **152 min**

Director:

Lewis Milestone

Writer:

George Abbott

Academy Awards:

For best director, production and best picture

A poster for *All Quiet on the Western Front*. Despite the film's popularity in the US, Hitler had it banned from cinemas in Germany due to its depiction of open defiance of military authority and perceived criticism of the Nazi regime.

An outstanding epic set on the Western Front in World War I, this is the first great 'talkie' war film. Based on the best-selling German novel of the same name by Erich Maria Remarque, it expresses a post-war reaction to the conflict, portraying the ordinary soldiers of both sides as the victims of incompetent and misguided commanders. It set the tone for many more such anti-war movies later in the century.

The opening title card makes clear that this film is 'neither an accusation nor a confession, and least of all an adventure, for death is not an adventure to those who stand face to face with it.' It is also about the continuing impact of the war on those who survived it. It begins dramatically with a door opening onto the war as we see German troops march to the front. A postman declares he is changing his uniform for that of an NCO and the music of the military band initially drowns out a teacher lecturing his students. It is this teacher who then encourages the whole class to join up for a 'quick war'. We follow the enthusiastic teenagers as they are put through their training by the former

The brutal reality of trench warfare forms an important part of the film. Here we see actor Lew Ayres and members of his squad scramble to put on their gas masks. Though often seen as an iconic image of World War I, the threat of death from mustard gas was actually very slim in comparison to infection or gangrene.

Actor Lew Ayres plays Paul Baumer, an idealistic young German boy who, after listening to an impassioned speech by his school teacher, decides to join the army in defence of the 'Fatherland'.

postman. They take exception to his harsh regime and dunk him in mud.

On the Western Front, the young men come under the influence of a cynical but fatherly veteran, played brilliantly by Louis Wolheim. The battle scenes are filmed on an epic scale as we see hundreds of French soldiers attack the German lines, only to face a brutal counter-attack that takes them all back to the same position. Machine guns mow down lines of men on both sides. One iconic scene shows the hero of the story, Paul Baumer, played by Lew Ayres, trapped in a shell crater where he stabs a French soldier. But the dying soldier lingers on through the night and Baumer is racked by guilt, saying 'Forgive me comrade.'

We see the reality of life in the trenches, with soldiers using spades to battle against rats. They question the value of the war and its commanders, saying that all the political leaders should settle their differences by fighting it out with clubs in a field. This open defiance of military authority made the film particularly unpopular in Nazi Germany, where Hitler had it banned. In the US, it won two Oscars and Steven Spielberg later claimed that Lewis Milestone's dynamic action scenes had an influence on his making of *Saving Private Ryan*.

Film number: **3**

LA GRANDE ILLUSION

Date: **1937**   Duration: **114 min**
Director:
Jean Renoir
Writers:
Jean Renoir, Charles Spaak

A poster for *La Grande Illusion* a film that is as much about class and common humanity as it is about World War I.

A French prisoner of war escape movie set in World War I, *La Grande Illusion* is in reality a socialist exploration of class and common humanity. From its beginning, in which we see captured French reconnaissance pilots treated to a generous lunch by the German fighter pilot who shot them down, this is a film about breaking down boundaries between nations. But the bonds of brotherhood depicted are largely between members of the same social class, especially between the two aristocratic officers, Captain de Boeldieu, played elegantly by Pierre Fresnay, and Rittmeister von Rauffenstein, performed by Erich von Stroheim in excellent Prussian style. The film takes its title from a British book about economic integration making war futile, by writer and Labour MP Norman Angell.

Covering similar anti-war themes as *All Quiet on the Western Front*, Renoir's film does so with far less attention to the brutal reality of war. Indeed, the scenes inside the German prisoner of war camp seem laughably relaxed with the Frenchmen dining comfortably on food parcels from Paris and sipping cognac. Even when the working class hero Lieutenant Maréchal, played by Jean Gabin, is put into solitary confinement, his German guard does everything he can to make him feel better. With such a jolly incarceration, it seems improbable

JEA
PIE
ERIC

JEAN

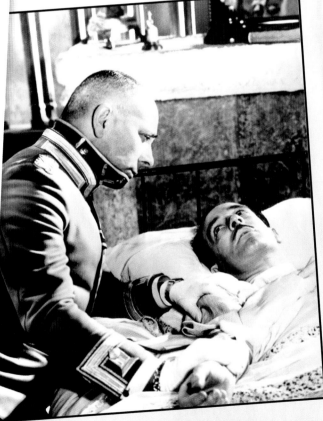

Erich von Stroheim and Pierre Fresnay in a scene from *La Grande Illusion* in which a German fighter pilot, Rittmeister von Rauffenstein, cares for his wounded French adversary after shooting him down.

they would want to escape and the process of building a tunnel is treated more as sport than a necessity.

Throughout the film, the Germans are portrayed sympathetically and there is barely any ill treatment of the French prisoners. It is little wonder that the French audience flocking to see this on the eve of World War II would think there was little to fear from German invasion and that defeat at their hands wouldn't be that bad. The sense of sharing a culture and values with the enemy is echoed in the British wartime movie *The Life and Death of Colonel Blimp*, but in that the true terrible nature of the Nazi regime is discussed. In *La Grande Illusion*, there is no reference to Nazism and the wealthy French Jewish character is the butt of jovial but nonetheless anti-Semitic comments. It is very much a film of its time and place and though an accomplished and enjoyable exercise in utopianism, it now seems a little naïve.

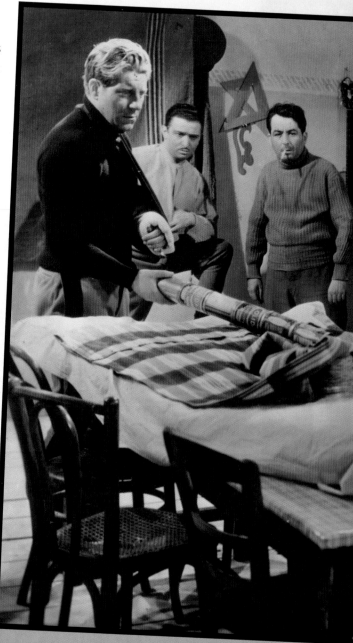

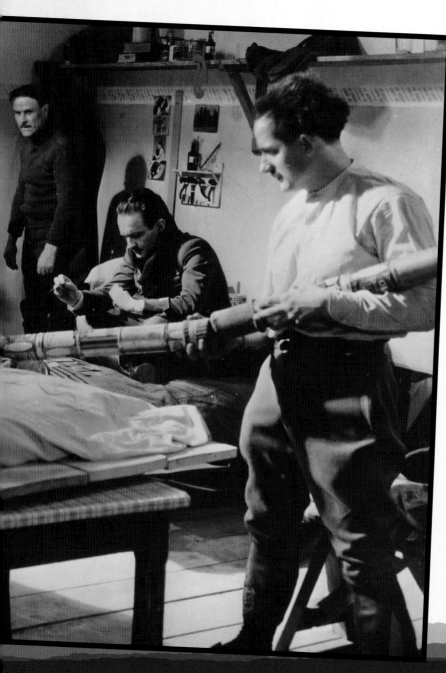

Unlike other related films of the 1930s, *La Grande Illusion* paid almost no attention to the brutal reality of war. Here we see French prisoners treating their attempts at escape as more sport than necessity.

Film number: **4**

SERGEANT YORK

Date: **1941**   Duration: **134 min**

Director:

Howard Hawks

Writers:

Abem Finkel, Harry Chandlee, Howard Koch, John Huston

Academy Awards:

For best actor, and best film editing

An enormously popular film – the highest grossing of 1941 – it coincided with the Japanese attack on Pearl Harbor and served as a very effective US recruiting tool. It tells the story of Alvin York, an American war hero of World War I, and was based on his diary. York refused several times to sell the film rights to his life story, until the producers promised that the money would go towards the funding of a Bible school.

Gary Cooper plays World War I hero Alvin York in *Sergeant York*. The real Alvin C York was one of the most highly decorated soldiers of World War I, receiving the Medal of Honor for his capture of a German machine-gun post during the Meuse-Argonne Offensive of 1918.

The film makes the most of York's humble Tennessee background, and Gary Cooper plays the lead role with immense charm. An expert marksman, he's a fighting and drinking young man until he meets the woman he falls in love with. He then works hard to buy a farm but is cheated out of it and goes back to alcohol. Stumbling into a church meeting after being struck by lightning, he has a religious awakening and tries to mend his ways. He initially avoids enlistment in 1917 because of his religious beliefs, but his church is not officially recognised, and so he is sent off for basic training. At the camp, his talent as a marksman is discovered and his superior officer tries to persuade York to fight abroad by referring to the sacrifices made by previous US soldiers in the defence of their homeland.

Publicity material for *Sergeant York*. The film was used as an effective propaganda and recruitment tool as it helped to sway many Americans who were unsure of entering another war in mainland Europe.

At home, a wind blows open his bible to the verse saying 'Render therefore unto Caesar the things which are Caesar's; and unto God the things that are God's.'

In France, York takes part in the Argonne Offensive and uses his shooting skills to capture a German machine-gun post. He then gets a captured German officer to order the surrender of other troops, capturing 132 prisoners in total. He is awarded the Medal of Honor and is given a ticker-tape parade through New York. But true to his Christian ethics, the humble York is not interested in commercial reward, taking no pride in his wartime achievements. He instead wants to go home – where his grateful community have bought him the farm he wanted. This heart-warming tale struck the right note for many Americans unsure about their involvement in another foreign war. It also inspired a young Clint Eastwood. 'One of the first films I went to' he recalled, 'was *Sergeant York*. My dad was a big admirer of Sergeant York stories from the First World War. It was directed by Howard Hawks. That was when I first became aware of movies, who made them, who was involved.'

The Meuse-Argonne Offensive of 1918 is an important part of *Sergeant York* and the film effectively portrays the horrors of trench warfare faced by all sides who fought in World War I.

Film number: **5**

IN WHICH WE SERVE

Date: **1942**   Duration: **115 min**

Directors:

Noel Coward, David Lean

Writer:

Noel Coward

Academy Award:

Honorary Academy Award for outstanding production achievement (Noel Coward)

A publicity poster for the film *In Which We Serve*. Despite the film's popularity at home and abroad in the US, many within the British Admiralty were less enthusiastic, dubbing it 'In Which We Sink'.

A stirring and touching tale of naval courage in World War II, written and directed by the celebrated playwright Noel Coward with the assistance of the British Ministry of Information. Dedicated to the Royal Navy, it was intended as a propaganda film and exemplifies the idea of a nation working together to defeat the enemy, setting aside class divisions in a shared endeavour.

'This is the story of a ship,' says the voiceover at the beginning of the film and we see the building of the destroyer HMS *Torrin* with steel plates riveted and the great hull assembled. It then cuts straight to the action in the Mediterranean in which the ship comes under fire from German bombers and, after a terrific fight, is sunk. Captain Kinross, played by Noel Coward, and the crew are cast into the sea, cling to a lifeboat and, in a series of flashbacks, we learn about the lives of the servicemen, their families and their wives.

Kinross makes it clear he wants to run a 'happy and efficient' ship and his paternal

Noel Coward as Captain Kinross. Despite his experience of directing plays Coward was new to the film industry and some, including the film studio, feared his persona was not quite suited to the role of a tough Navy captain.

role is demonstrated by the way he treats his crew with discipline and humanity. Richard Attenborough makes his first screen appearance as a rating who loses his nerve in battle. The supporting role of wives in the war effort is expressed by actress Celia Johnson, who makes an elegant speech accepting that her rival in love will always be her husband's ship. Coward's trademark wit is on display with some funny interchanges, especially when the crew listen to the radio broadcast of Prime Minister Chamberlain expressing disappointment on the outbreak of war – 'Isn't exactly a big holiday for us,' snaps back 'Shorty' Blake, played by John Mills.

Coward was inspired to write the story by the sinking of HMS *Kelly* during the battle for Crete in 1941. The ship's commander was Lord Louis Mountbatten and he lent his support to the making of the film. Coward used Mountbatten's speech to the survivors of the *Kelly* for the finale of the film. The realistic action scenes were directed by a young David Lean and are full of fascinating detail and tremendous noise, including the ever present throbbing of the ship's great engines. HMS *Torrin* is, of course, a metaphor for the British island nation and the film ends with a new ship being launched and Kinross in command of his own battleship.

The sinking of HMS *Torrin* is a crucial moment in the film and Coward was determined for British audiences not to view it as a defeat, but instead the first step on a journey towards victory against Germany.

MRS MINIVER

Date: 1942   **Duration: 133 min**

Director:

William Wyler

Writers:

Arthur Wimperis, George Froeschel, James Hilton, Claudine West

Academy Awards:

For best picture, best director, best actress (Greer Garson), best supporting actress (Teresa Wright), best screenplay, and best cinematography (Joseph Ruttenberg)

A moving drama about the 'Home Front' in World War II, *Mrs Miniver* communicated effectively to an American audience the sacrifice being made by families in Britain suffering from German bombing. Seen through the eyes of a comfortable middle class housewife, played superbly by Greer Garson, living in a 'quiet corner of England', it makes the point that everyone is vulnerable in a total war and each makes their own contribution.

Greer Garson as Mrs Miniver. Her touching performance in this wartime classic won her an Academy Award for best actress. The film collected five more Academy Awards and is still hailed as one of the most inspirational films of all time.

VOTED THE GREATEST MOVIE MADE!

GREER GARSON
Walter PIDGEON

WILLIAM WYLER Produced by SIDNEY FRANKLIN

MRS. MINIVER

with
TERESA WRIGHT · DAME MAY WHITTY
REGINALD OWEN · HENRY TRAVERS
RICHARD NEY · HENRY WILCOXON
SCREEN PLAY BY ARTHUR WIMPERIS, GEORGE FROESCHEL, JAMES HILTON AND CLAUDINE WEST

WILLIAM WYLER PRODUCTION
BASED ON JAN STRUTHER

When the film begins, Mrs Miniver's biggest worry is about whether she ought to buy an expensive hat she has taken a fancy to. Her husband, played by Walter Pidgeon, has his own sense of guilt about splashing out on a new car. Then there is controversy about whether a rose named after Mrs Miniver can be allowed to enter the local village competition that has always been dominated by the fierce Lady Beldon and her roses. This vision of an idyllic Britain is shattered by the outbreak of war and Mrs Miniver's son immediately joins the RAF as a pilot. He proposes to Lady Beldon's granddaughter and they hastily marry because in war 'time is so precious'.

A poster for the 1940s movie *Mrs Miniver*. The film deliberately focused on the plight of British families during World War II in the hope it would sway public opinion, particularly in America, in favour of intervention against Germany.

An impressive scene shows numerous little boats gathering to help evacuate British soldiers from the beaches of Dunkirk, but while her husband is one of the civilians helping with the rescue, Mrs Miniver is placed on the front line of the aerial war when she is confronted by an aggressive, wounded Luftwaffe pilot. A bombing raid is frighteningly reconstructed, with Mrs Miniver and her family huddling in a shelter in their garden. 'Mummy, they nearly killed us this time,' says one of their little children. The intensely touching ending underlines that this is a 'war of all the people'.

Unsurprisingly, the film was an immense popular success and won six Oscars. Part of the script was quickly re-written following the attack on Pearl Harbor and America's entry into the war, making it more uncompromising in its stance against the enemy. The final speech delivered by the vicar in the film was quoted in propaganda leaflets dropped on Nazi Europe. The brother of the actor playing the vicar, Henry Wilcoxon, had been killed during the Dunkirk evacuation, making his words of defiance even more poignant: 'This is the People's War. It is our war. We are the fighters.'

The famous scene from *Mrs Miniver* in which the vicar of Belham delivers his sermon within the damaged ruins of their local parish church. His speech was used in real propaganda leaflets dropped on Nazi Germany.

THE LIFE AND DEATH OF COLONEL BLIMP

Date: **1943**   Duration: **163 min**

Directors:

Michael Powell,
Emeric Pressburger

Writers:

Michael Powell,
Emeric Pressburger

A poster for *The Life and Death of Colonel Blimp*. The film was shot in vivid Technicolor and remains a favourite of many acclaimed filmmakers, such as Martin Scorsese, to this day.

The Life and Death of Colonel Blimp is an immensely touching movie and yet curious too, especially considering that it was made during the middle of World War II. It is really a love story that deals with Britishness and whether its values of fair play are suited to the struggle against Adolf Hitler. It captures an Edwardian affection for German culture and could only really have been made before the revelations of Nazi genocide at the end of the war. British wartime leader Winston Churchill was not a fan of the film and wanted it banned, with some historians claiming he feared the main character was a caricature of himself.

Named after cartoons by David Low, making fun of an old fashioned military gentleman, the film begins with the apparently Blimpish character, Major General Clive Wynne-Candy – played by Roger Livesey – being outwitted by younger military officers. We then see Candy's military career through a series of flashbacks. On leave from the Boer War in 1902, Candy visits Berlin to meet his friend Edith, played by Deborah Kerr. She complains that the Germans are spreading anti-British propaganda

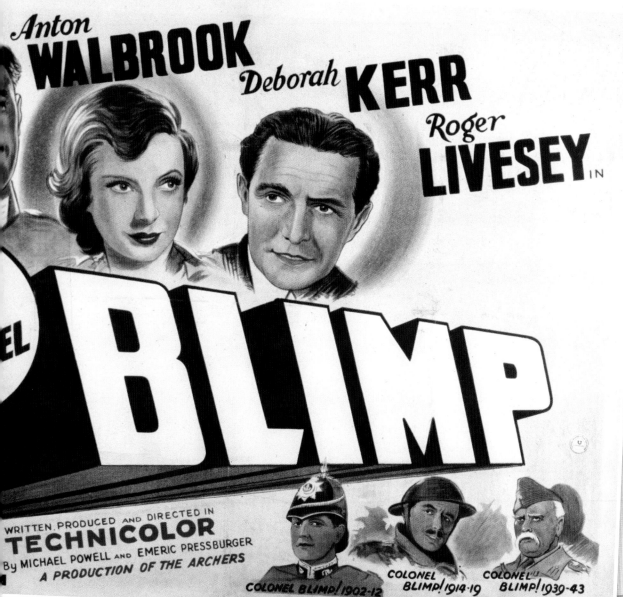

and Candy fights a duel with a German officer, Theo Kretschmar-Schuldorff, played by Anton Walbrook. While recovering from their wounds, the two become good friends and Kretschmar proposes to Edith. Too late, Candy realises he loves Edith.

At the end of World War I, Candy and Kretschmar resume their friendship and in 1939 Kretschmar comes to England, where Candy reveals his love for Edith. Restored to military service, Candy is appalled by the brutality of the German blitzkrieg and declares he'd rather see Britain lose the war than apply the same ruthless tactics used by the Nazis. Kretschmar argues that any methods are acceptable in the fight against Hitler. 'If you preach the Rules of the Game while they use every foul and filthy trick against you, they will laugh at you!' he says.

The film was shot in vivid Technicolor and its style seems more akin to the anti-war movies of the 1960s. Many of its shots have a 'pop' quality to them, such as the scene in which Candy's wall fills with animal trophies, each one appearing to the sound of a gunshot. Many great filmmakers have acclaimed it, including Martin Scorsese, who raised funds for its restoration.

FAR LEFT Roger Livesey as Major General Clive Wynne-Candy. While the film is decidedly pro-British, Candy's likeness to Winston Churchill and its satire of the British Army and its leadership angered the Prime Minister, who is said to have wanted the film's production stopped.

LEFT Anton Walbrook in a publicity still for *The Life and Death of Colonel Blimp*. Walbrook's character, Theo Kretschmar-Schuldorff, is Candy's chief rival for the affection of Edith, the film's leading female and shared love interest, played by Deborah Kerr.

Film number: **8**

TWELVE O'CLOCK HIGH

Date: **1949**   Duration: **132 min**
Director:
Henry King
Writers:
Sy Bartlett, Beirne Lay Jr
Academy Awards:
For best supporting actor
(Dean Jagger), and sound recording

A poster of the 1940s film *Twelve O'Clock High*. Though nominated for four Academy Awards, the film only received two, despite its popularity with critics, the general public and service personnel.

A hard-hitting, straight-talking film about a collapse in morale in a US Army Air Force daylight precision bombing group. 'These were the only Americans fighting in Europe in the fall of 1942,' says the opening title card. 'They stood alone, against the enemy and against doubts from home and abroad.' Gregory Peck plays the USAAF general given the task of rebuilding their discipline and fighting spirit, but this complex film shows how challenging that is.

The film begins in London in 1949 when a former USAAF major, played by Dean Jagger, spies a Toby jug in a shop that awakens his memories of the war. He revisits the dilapidated former Archbury air base surrounded by the English countryside. As he walks on the overgrown runway, he hears the roar of aircraft engines and we cut back to 1942 to see US B-17 bombers landing. One crash lands and out of the craft tumbles a crew traumatised by their mission. One pilot vomits, having been struggling for two hours to gain the controls from another pilot who's had the back of his head shot off. The severed arm of another badly injured pilot remains in the craft. It is a no-nonsense introduction to the high losses endured by daytime bomber crews. The unit's morale is further undermined by a well-informed Nazi propaganda broadcast by Lord Haw-Haw – a nickname for the German wartime broadcaster William Joyce – that taunts the Americans for undertaking risky daylight bombing

raids over Europe. The next day, 28 crewmen ask to be excused from their next raid. It exposes a crisis in morale.

'How much can a man take?' asks their medical officer. 'The rules say a man goes unless he'll endanger his crew' comes the response from Group Commander Davenport, played by Gary Merrill. But even his determination is shaken by the prospect of their next low-flying mission and he is relieved of his command because he has identified too strongly with the plight of his men. His place is taken by Brigadier

A publicity still of Gregory Peck in *Twelve O'Clock High*. The character of Brigadier General Frank Savage was actually based on a number of different USAAF group commanders who fought in World War II, most notably Colonel Frank A Armstrong, the famous leader of the 306th Bomb Group.

General Frank Savage, played by Peck, and most of the film is about his efforts to rebuild the morale of his pilots. At one point, he establishes a separate aircraft for the men that have failed him most – dubbed the 'Leper Colony' – but that is the craft he pilots when he joins his men on their next missions over France and Germany. The film is an extraordinary study of the psychology of servicemen and was quite rightly acclaimed at the time, and later used by the USAAF for the purpose of leadership training. The aerial battle scenes towards the end of the film are edited from actual combat footage from the USAAF and Luftwaffe.

The film's directors went to great lengths in order to provide realistic aerial battle scenes, especially towards the latter stages of the film, where edited footage of actual USAAF and Luftwaffe engagements was used.

SANDS OF IWO JIMA

Date: **1949**   Duration: **100 min**

Director:

Allan Dwan

Writers:

Harry Brown, James Edward Grant

A gritty film about the US Pacific War made just four years after the end of World War II. Hollywood Western star John Wayne plays the tough US Marine Sergeant Stryker leading his troops against the Japanese during the island-hopping campaign. 'Saddle up!' he says as they go into action.

John Wayne as US Marine Sergeant Stryker, a tough, uncompromising leader who eventually wins the respect of his men as they fight through a series of bloody battles on the US Pacific front.

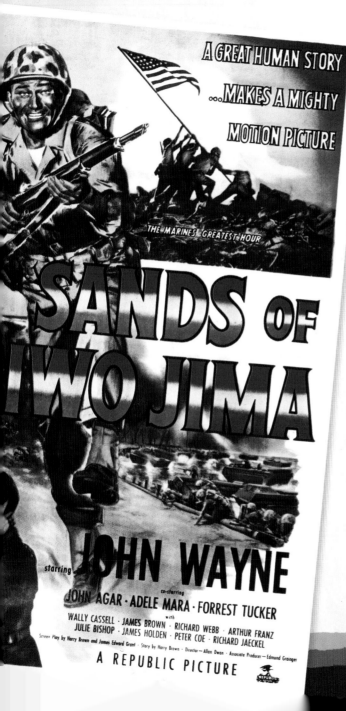

Stryker knocks his new recruits into shape straight after Guadalcanal, but not everyone likes his harsh style and Private Conway, the college educated son of a much-respected Colonel, played by John Agar, makes it clear. So does Private Thomas, played by Forrest Tucker, an army boxing champion beaten by Stryker. The Rifle Squad faces its first ordeal as its hits the beaches of Tarawa and Thomas lets down his colleagues, with one of them dying. Stryker confronts him and punches him, but when they are seen fighting by a superior officer, Thomas defends Stryker, saying they were merely practising judo. He is relieved to unburden his guilty conscience. It is one of several incidents that prove the value of Stryker's leadership and by the end of the film

The original poster for the film *Sands of Iwo Jima*. The famous raising of the US flag atop Mount Suribachi by three US Marines is clearly visible in the upper half of the image.

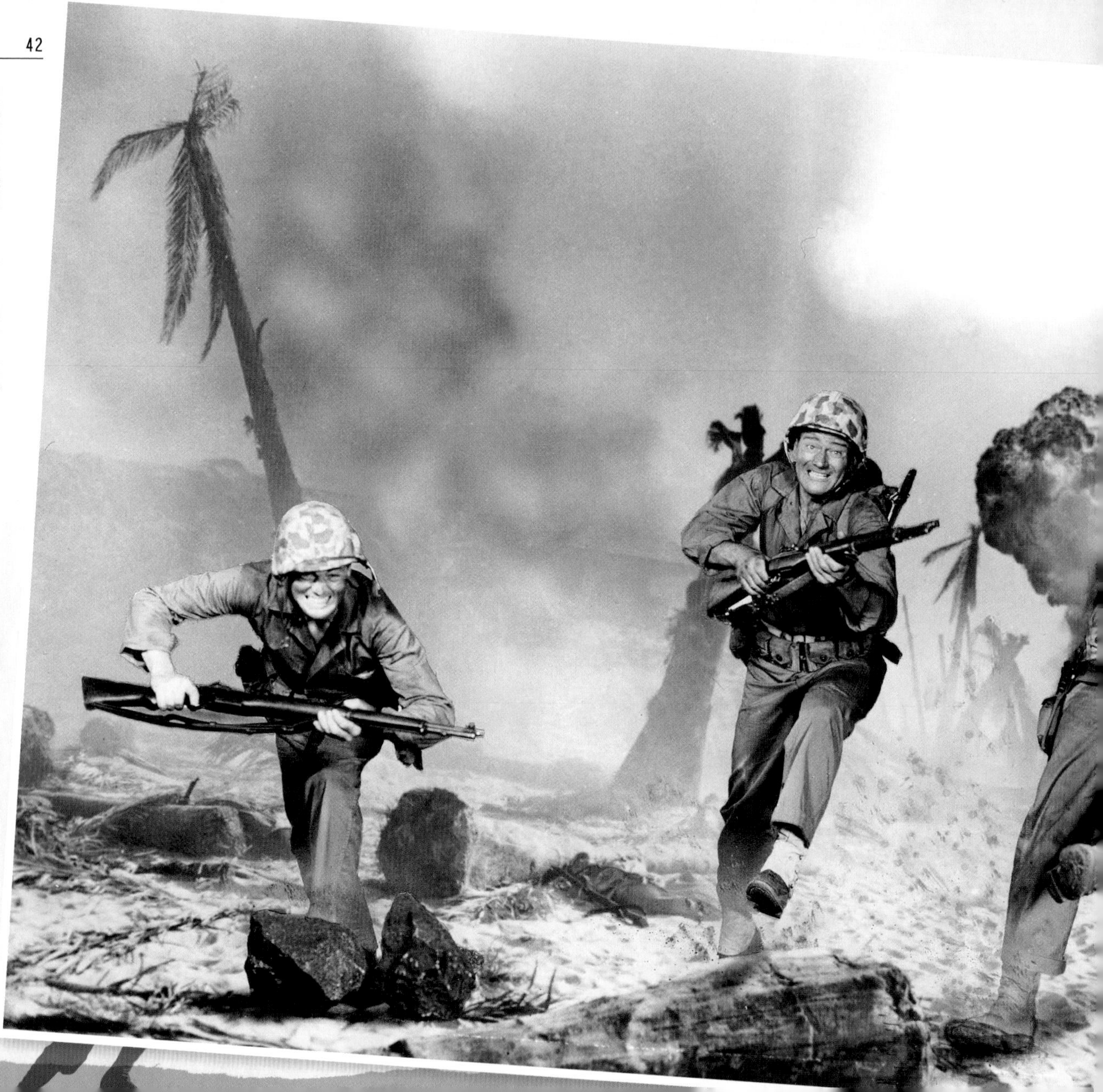

his men respect him. But Stryker is tormented by his own demons – he has split from his wife and yearns for a letter from his 10-year-old son. On leave, he constantly gets drunk but when he meets a single mother working as a bar girl, he does the right thing and gives her some money for food for her child.

The storyline is interspersed with epic battle scenes featuring the full panoply of beach assault weaponry, including flame-throwing tanks and hundreds of US Marine extras. It also is spliced with real war footage. The Marine Rifle Squad takes part in the landing at Iwo Jima and there is a recreation of the iconic raising of the US flag on Mount Suribachi. Three of the actual servicemen who raised the flag – Rene Gagnon, Ira Hayes and John Bradley – appear briefly in the film as Wayne gives them the flag. The script is claimed to be the first film use of the phrase 'lock and load'.

Unlike many other Hollywood war film actors Wayne did not serve his country during the war. At the time of Pearl Harbor he was 34 and considered too old, and he was dissuaded from later attempts to enlist by the studios that did not want to lose one of their top earning stars. He did tour US bases in the Pacific during the war and regretted not serving.

Grand battle scenes form an important part of *Sands of Iwo Jima* and the film's director employed a full complement of beach assault weaponry, tanks and hundreds of US Marines to give these reenactments the authenticity they deserved.

THE STEEL HELMET

Date: **1951**   Duration: **85 min**

Director:

Samuel Fuller

Writer:

Samuel Fuller

A poster for *The Steel Helmet*. The film's director and writer, Samuel Fuller, used his script as a platform from which to criticise the racism endemic in 1950s America and to explore the brutality of war, all of which deeply angered the Pentagon and FBI.

Fuller was adamant that the lead role of Sergeant Zack should be played by Gene Evans (left), turning down offers from other studios to cast more famous actors such as John Wayne and Larry Parks.

The first Hollywood film about the Korean War, *The Steel Helmet* was made by a World War II veteran who didn't hold back on the uncomfortable aspects of war. It opens with the massacre of US prisoners of war by the North Koreans and a close-up of a bullet-holed M1 helmet. Slowly, we see the helmet rise to reveal the only survivor of the slaughter, Sergeant Zack, played by Gene Evans. The helmet becomes a talisman throughout the movie, but does not deliver the luck it should.

A local boy, played by William Chun, rescues the sergeant by cutting the cords that bind his hands. The boy has lost both his parents to the Communist onslaught and attaches himself to Zack. When the gruff Zack calls him a 'gook', he proudly rebuffs him, saying he is a Korean. Zack dubs him 'Short Round' and he earns the sergeant's respect and affection. They then link up with an African-American medic and this is the first of several encounters that allows Samuel Fuller, who was both the film's director and writer, to mention the racism

that is endemic in 1950s America. A Japanese-American veteran of World War II is taunted by a Communist prisoner over his loyalty to a country that interned his family while he fought the Nazis in Europe. But the overriding message of the film is that there are basic rules of behaviour, even in war, and the Americans strive not to break them, as shown by their determination to treat with great respect a Buddhist temple they capture as an observation post. In contrast, the Communist North Koreans violate these standards. At one point, the idealistic officer orders a soldier to retrieve the identity dog tags from a dead American, but the body is booby-trapped and he is blown up.

Occasionally a little too stagey, the film wears its liberal credentials clearly and as a result irritated the military establishment at the time. It also provoked an investigation into the director by the FBI, but the film certainly does not portray the Communists in a good light. When challenged about the shooting of an unarmed prisoner of war, Fuller argued that this had happened several times during his service in the army and it is clearly shown to be wrong. Made on a shoe-string budget with student extras and a plywood tank, it made a huge profit at the box office. Fuller went on to make several more war films, including *The Big Red One*.

A scene showing Sergeant Zack and his ragtag band of American soldiers as they advance towards what they believe to be an abandoned Buddhist temple.

Film number: **11**

THE CRUEL SEA

Date: **1953**   Duration: **126 min**
Director:
Charles Frend
Writer:
Eric Ambler

A drama about a Royal Navy warship protecting British convoys against German submarine attacks in World War II, *The Cruel Sea* tells the story of the ship's crew and the challenges they face at sea. The opening shots of mountainous dark waves are followed by scenes of the ship plunging through rough seas, spray drenching the crew, making it clear that the sea is as much an enemy as the German U-boats.

Jack Hawkins (right) plays Lieutenant Commander Ericson, a man haunted by the difficult decisions he is forced to make at sea.

A movie poster for *The Cruel Sea*. Much like the film's opening moments this poster draws attention to the dark, dangerous nature of the ocean.

Jack Hawkins plays Lieutenant Commander Ericson, a naval reserve officer put in charge of a team of inexperienced young officers. His men have barely been at sea – one is a banker, another was a second-hand car salesman just a few weeks before – but as they face their first missions and conflicts, they mature and become an effective force. Much of the group's time is spent rescuing merchant seamen from ships sunk in their convoy. There are tense moments when they have to stop the ship, making it a sitting target for enemy torpedoes. In a voice-over, Hawkins grimly describes what they learn: 'You knew how to keep watch on filthy nights, and how to go without sleep, how to bury the dead, and how to die without wasting anyone's time.'

When they finally do pick up a signal of a nearby submarine on their ASDIC detection device (known to the Americans as sonar), Ericson faces the terrible choice of having to unleash depth charges while there are still sailors to be rescued swimming around in the sea above the target. His decision haunts him throughout the film but other merchant

seamen he has saved tell him how much they appreciate his help. He concludes 'no one murdered them, it's the war.'

Part of the film follows the lives of the crew on leave and there are tragic moments when the war impacts on the 'Home Front'. A row of terraced houses by the docks gets badly bombed. One officer, played by Denholm Elliott, is married to a London showgirl who cheats on him while he is away.

The film was based on the best-selling book of the same name by Nicholas Monsarrat, a former journalist and naval reserve veteran of the battle of the Atlantic. The ship featured in the film, *Compass Rose*, was a Flower-class corvette specialising in anti-submarine duties, being armed with a 4-inch gun, a 2-pounder pom-pom gun and racks of depth charges. The film was the most popular British movie of 1953 and confirmed Jack Hawkins as a major star.

Many of the open water scenes like the one seen here were shot at Denham Studios, in a massive open-air water tank. However, the actor Donald Sinden could not swim, adding a real element of danger to each take.

THE DAM BUSTERS

Date: **1955**   Duration: **124 min**

Director:

Michael Anderson

Writer:

R C Sherriff

A poster for *The Dam Busters*, a film about the wartime raids conducted by the RAF's famous 617 Squadron against three dams in Germany along the Ruhr Valley. The pilots used the ingenious bouncing bomb, which could skim across the surface of water like a pebble, to destroy their targets.

The ultimate war film combining backroom ingenuity with frontline bravery, it tells the World War II story of the raid by RAF 617 Squadron against three dams in Germany crucial to the Nazi war effort. It was – and remains – unusual as a war film for devoting much of the screen time to military invention, as aviation engineer Barnes Wallis, played by Michael Redgrave, devises a bomb that will skip across the water like a pebble in front

A scene showing Robert Shaw as Flight Sergeant John Pulford (left), and Richard Todd as Wing Commander Guy Gibson (right), in their Lancaster bomber.

of the dams. His numerous failures – many in front of the government ministers funding the experiments – plunge him into despair and doubt about the project. When he manages to get the support of RAF Bomber Command's Sir Arthur Harris and the green light from Prime Minister Churchill, it then finally becomes a military operation under the leadership of celebrated pilot Guy Gibson, played by Richard Todd.

Gibson selects an elite squadron of Lancaster bomber pilots and they practise low flying above British lakes, much to the consternation of at least one local farmer, who writes a letter complaining about the noise of the aircraft triggering his hens to lay premature eggs. The bouncing bomb is not the only technical problem to be solved and Gibson gets inspiration for a device to calculate low flying at a precise height from visiting the theatre and watching shafts of light from spotlights meet on the stage. This was one of the few dramatic aspects of the film that was not in fact true, the light altimeter having been used previously by RAF Coastal Command. Real Lancaster bombers were used for the action sequences alongside actual test footage of the

bombs, but technical aspects of the bomb were disguised, as details of the 1943 operation – only just over a decade before the making of the film – were still classified.

The film was an immediate popular success with a British audience hungry to learn of the secret technical war against Nazi Germany. But pride in the triumph of the bouncing bomb is very much tempered at the end of the film by the sombre appreciation that 56 pilots did not return from the successful mission. The stirring music from the film's soundtrack, *The Dam Busters March*, composed by Eric Coates, has helped to maintain its popularity. However, since 1955 changing sensibilities has made the frequent mention of Guy Gibson's dog 'Nigger' an awkward moment for broadcasters, as the 'N-word' is also used as code for a successful bombing run in the film.

A combination of wartime footage and real Lancaster bombers, all four of which were supplied by the RAF, were used for the aerial sequences, and different locations across the UK, such as the Upper Derwent Valley in Derbyshire, substituted for the Ruhr in Germany.

THE BRIDGE ON THE RIVER KWAI

Date: **1957**   Duration: **161 min**

Director:

David Lean

Writers:

Carl Foreman, Michael Wilson

Academy Awards:

For best picture, director, screenplay, actor (Alec Guinness), cinematography (Jack Hildyard), original score, and film editing.

A poster for *The Bridge on the River Kwai*. The film was loosely based on the notorious Burma–Siam railway, otherwise known as the Death Railway, built during World War II. Some 13,000 Commonwealth, American and Dutch prisoners lost their lives during its construction.

"A MAGNIFICENT, MOVING FILM!"
LIFE Magazine

"DESTINED TO BECOME A CLASSIC!"
LOOK Magazine

COLUMBIA PICTURES presents
A SAM SPIEGEL PRODUCTION

WILLIAM HOLDEN
ALEC GUINNESS
JACK HAWKINS

"THE BRIDGE ON THE RIVER KWAI"

TECHNICOLOR
CinemaScope

with SESSUE HAYAKAWA · JAMES DONALD · ANN SEARS and introducing GEOFFREY HORNE · Directed by DAVID LEAN · Screenplay by PIERRE BOULLE Based on his Novel

A prisoner of war drama set in Japanese occupied Burma, this film is notable for the performance of Alec Guinness as the captured British officer obsessed with building a bridge for his Japanese captors. The film is based on the French language novel by Pierre Boulle, who also wrote *Planet of the Apes*, and was a prisoner of the Japanese in World War II and used his experiences as a slave labourer in the original story.

Alec Guinness stars as Lieutenant Colonel Nicholson, a British officer captured in Japanese occupied Burma. This memorable performance is often seen as one of the best of his career and won him an Academy Award for Best Actor.

The film begins with the British prisoners marching into the camp to the famous sound of the Colonel Bogey march and being told they are to build a bridge over the river Kwai linking Thailand to Burma. At first, Lieutenant Colonel Nicholson, played by Guinness, tells the Japanese prison commander, Colonel Saito, played by Sessue Hayakawa, that according to the Geneva Convention, officers are exempt from such labour. There then follows a battle of wills as the officers are left standing in the blazing sun. Nicholson is slapped by Saito and singled out for punishment in an iron box, but refuses to give in.

Faced with failure, Saito compromises and releases Nicholson and his officers. Until that point, the other men have been sabotaging the building project, but – and this is where the film takes a strange but brilliant turn – Nicholson decides that his men's morale is better served by constructing the best bridge they can. Some of the other officers protest that this is collaborating with the enemy, but Nicholson becomes obsessed with it, believing the bridge will demonstrate the superiority of British engineering skill. His pride in the work gives the film's spectacular finale a tremendous emotional hit.

Guinness's gaunt, troubled portrayal is one of the best of his career and won him an Oscar. The film was a massive commercial hit and critically acclaimed, setting up David Lean perfectly for his next big war drama, *Lawrence of Arabia*. The film was shot in Sri Lanka and even though tourists today are taken to see a bridge over the river Kwai in northern Thailand, the river was in fact renamed in the 1960s to make it a tourist site. Nonetheless, parts of this bridge were built by prisoners of war in 1943. Some 13,000 captured servicemen died working on the Death Railway and their conditions were much worse than those portrayed in the film.

William Holden as USN Commander Shears, the only officer to escape his Japanese captors in the film. Though badly wounded, he is eventually helped by some local villagers and placed on a boat to freedom.

Film number: **14**

PATHS OF GLORY

Date: **1957**   Duration: **88 min**

Director:

Stanley Kubrick

Writers:

Stanley Kubrick, Calder Willingham,
Jim Thompson

A poster for *Paths of Glory*.
Though the film received
great critical acclaim upon its
release in December 1957,
many French retired and
active personnel expressed
anger at Kubrick's portrayal of
the French Army and its
leaders during World War I
– a feeling shared by their
government who prevented
its release in French cinemas
until 1975.

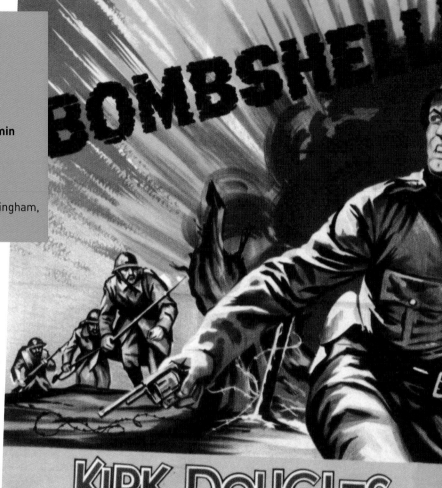

A strident study on the injustice of war, it tells the story of a failed assault by a French regiment in World War I, resulting in three soldiers being randomly accused of cowardice and facing death by execution. Kirk Douglas stars as Colonel Dax, a peacetime barrister, who steps in to defend his soldiers, one of whom had been previously decorated for bravery.

The film begins with two generals meeting in a beautifully decorated chateau. They discuss the need for an attack on an impregnable German position, dubbed the 'Anthill', despite knowing that casualties will be high and that there is little support to offer for the assault. On the front line, a drunken lieutenant shows cowardice during a reconnaissance mission, killing one of his own men, and later denies the accusations of the corporal who accompanied him. The corporal will be one of the men selected for execution. The assault itself on the Anthill is brilliantly directed by a young Kubrick, including one long tracking scene following Dax as he walks along lines of trenches encouraging his men. The sense of injustice is given a further twist when the French general in command orders his artillery to fire on a section of his men that have not left their trench. The court scene that follows allows Dax to give full vent to

OPPOSITE A scene showing scores of French soldiers rushing from their trenches as the attack on the 'Anthill', the infamous German fortified position, begins. Not a single man reaches the German trenches and an enraged General Mireau orders French artillery to fire on his own men.

Kirk Douglas as Colonel Dax, a barrister by trade, who bravely defends his soldiers against accusations of cowardice which carry the penalty of death.

his anger: 'The attack yesterday morning was no stain on the honour of France, and certainly no disgrace to the fighting men of this nation. But this court martial is such a stain, and such a disgrace.'

The use of execution to encourage the exertions of soldiers in World War I was widely practised by the Allies and the film is based on a particular French case of four soldiers executed in 1915 for failing to follow orders. Kubrick acquired the film rights to the novel of the same title, written by Humphrey Cobb. It was only when Kirk Douglas – then a major box office draw – showed interest in the script that a film was made. It was not a commercial success but was critically acclaimed. The French government was not so impressed and it was not released in France until 1975.

Film number: **15**

ICE COLD IN ALEX

Date: **1958**   Duration: **130 min**

Director:

J Lee Thompson

Writers:

Christopher Landon, T J Morrison

A desert survival tale set in World War II, it is most famous for being a film title about a long-awaited cool beer in Alexandria. Based on a novel by Christopher Landon, it is a darker tale than the usual *Boy's Own* glory movies of the period just after the war. The director J Lee Thompson would have great success with the action thriller *The Guns of Navarone*, three years later, but the hero of this film is a battle-stressed alcoholic, the British Captain Anson, played by John Mills.

Alongside John Mills, Sylvia Syms plays Sister Diana Murdoch, one of two nurses that accompany Mills as they attempt to drive their Austin K2/Y ambulance – nicknamed 'Katy' – across the treacherous sand dunes of the Qattara Depression.

Publicity poster for *Ice Cold in Alex*. The film was nominated for a BAFTA, and the Golden Berlin Bear and FIPRESCI Awards at the Berlin International Film Festival.

After being attacked by the Germans at Tobruk, Anson and his comrades, including two nurses, decide to drive an ambulance across the desert to Alexandria in Egypt. On the way they pick up a South African officer, Captain Van der Poele, played by Anthony Quayle. Anson keeps himself going through the journey by promising himself an ice-cold lager in 'Alex'. Van der Poele gets friendly with Anson by giving him a bottle of gin from his large backpack, but soon the British become suspicious of what he is really carrying in the sack. The group faces many challenges, including the treacherous sand dunes of the Qattara Depression – the film was actually shot in Libya. Van der Poele helps them with his tremendous physical strength when their ambulance gets bogged down. Because he is an Afrikaner, he speaks German to the Afrika Korps soldiers they come across, but that only deepens everyone's suspicion about his true motives. Their primary enemy, however, is the desert

and so any confrontation is put off by their need to work together as a team to survive.

The film reaches its climax in Alexandria when the exhausted team walk into a bar and Anson finally orders the cool drink he has been dreaming of. The classic scene has been parodied many times and featured in a popular Carlsberg beer advert in the 1980s. The original beer chosen in the film was in fact the Danish Carlsberg because the film-makers didn't want to use a German beer, and it is clearly recognisable from the glass. Thus, the beer advertisers only had to make a slight variation on their usual tag-line, saying '*Still* probably the best lager in the world.' Because John Mills was drinking real beer in the scene, after fourteen takes, he got quite drunk.

Perhaps the most famous scene in *Ice Cold in Alex* where British Captain Anson finally gets his glass of ice-cold lager at a bar in Alexandria.

LAWRENCE OF ARABIA

Date: **1962**   Duration: **227 min**

Director:

David Lean

Writers:

Robert Bolt, Michael Wilson

Academy Awards:

For best picture, director, art direction, cinematography (Frederick A Young), original score, film editing, and sound

A film poster for the epic movie *Lawrence of Arabia* about the Arab uprising in Ottoman Turkish territory in World War I.

After five years...the first motion picture from the cre...
Columbia Pictures presents The SAM SPIEG...

LAWRENCE O

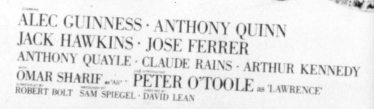

ALEC GUINNESS · ANTHONY QUINN
JACK HAWKINS · JOSE FERRER
ANTHONY QUAYLE · CLAUDE RAINS · ARTHUR KENNEDY
OMAR SHARIF as 'Ali' · PETER O'TOOLE as 'LAWRENCE'
ROBERT BOLT   SAM SPIEGEL · DAVID LEAN

Bridge On The River Kwai."

LEAN Production of

ARABIA

SUPER PANAVISION 70° · TE

An epic film about a relatively obscure theatre of conflict in World War I, it tells the story of T E Lawrence, a junior British officer who ends up leading an Arab revolt against the Ottoman Turks. Somewhat of a misfit in the British Army, his frankness endears him to Prince Faisal and he urges the Arab leader to attack Aqaba, a port that would allow the British to deliver military supplies to the Arabs. Lawrence wins the respect of the Arabs by surviving a journey through a harsh desert and they present him with Arab robes to wear. Their assault on Aqaba is a success and Lawrence is given arms and money to recruit the Arabs to fight alongside the British against the Turks.

Sir Alec Guinness as Prince Faisal, leader of the 1916–1918 Arab revolt and an instrumental figure in the history of what was then known as the Arab Kingdom of Syria. Guinness took his role very seriously and dedicated much time to the perfection of his accent.

The story is really about how one man can enter an alien land and through sheer force of personality become a respected military leader. It touches upon the same themes explored in *The Man Who Would be King*, the 1975 film based on Rudyard Kipling's tale about two adventurers in India, but this is not a satire of western imperialism and pursues the true story with epic grandeur, portraying the magnificence of the landscape and the scale of the achievement. Peter O'Toole shines in the part as the blond-haired Lawrence, an intellectual troubled by the violence he encounters and yet bewitched by it too. Ultimately, his loyalties are torn between his new Arab comrades and the British.

Sources for the film include Lawrence's autobiography, *The Seven Pillars of Wisdom*, and the articles of Lowell Thomas, an American

journalist whose reports about Lawrence made him an international hero after the war. The iconic photograph of him wearing Bedouin robes helped too. Historical criticism of the film says that an emphasis on the romance of the desert means that many of the Arab soldiers are shown as Bedouin irregulars when in fact most of them wore khaki uniforms.

The exterior shots were filmed in Jordan, Morocco, and Spain. Despite its length – it was screened in two halves with an interval – the film was a tremendous box office hit and has been acclaimed as one of the greatest movies ever made, inspiring leading directors such as George Lucas, Ridley Scott and Steven Spielberg.

Peter O'Toole plays the archaeologist, diplomat and British military officer T E Lawrence, better known as Lawrence of Arabia. His impassioned performance is lauded to this very day and, at the time, earned him an Academy Award nomination for Best Actor, a BAFTA for Best British Actor and a Golden Globe for Most Promising Newcomer.

Film number: **17**

THE LONGEST DAY

Date: **1962**   Duration: **169 min**

Directors:

Ken Annakin, Andrew Marton, Bernhard Wicki

Writer:

Cornelius Ryan

Academy Awards:

For best cinematography (Jean Bourgoin & Walter Wottitz), and best special effects (Robert MacDonald & Jacques Maumont)

Publicity material for *The Longest Day* emphasising the great number of international stars appearing in the movie. The artwork views the action from inside a German bunker, part of the defences at D-Day.

Very much intended as a spectacular star-studded epic, the film boasted 43 internationally recognised leading actors in its cast and part of the pleasure of watching it is identifying the famous faces: Sean Connery as a tough Irish soldier on Juno Beach, the role he played before becoming James Bond; Richard Burton as a wounded RAF pilot parachuting into Normandy; John Wayne as an 82nd Airborne officer leading his men into action despite a broken ankle; Henry Fonda as the 57-year-old son of former President Teddy Roosevelt insisting on taking his men in on the first assault at Utah Beach.

Each cameo part was based on a real military figure identified in Cornelius Ryan's 1959 best-selling book of the same name, which skilfully wove the true stories of D-Day veterans into a narrative describing the entire operation. Producer Darryl F Zanuck paid Cornelius Ryan $175,000 for the film rights and he wrote most of the screenplay too. There are some extraordinary set-piece scenes such as the aerial shot tracking hundreds

NCLUDING:— EDDIE ALBE
RAY DANTON ▪ IRINA
JEFFREY HUNTER ▪ CU
MICHAEL MEDWIN ▪ S
RON RANDELL ▪ NORM
TOM TRYON ▪

RYL F. ZANUCK'S

THE LONGEST DAY A

From the book by CORNELIUS RYAN
Released by 20th CENTURY-FOX

INTERNATIONAL STARS

KA ▪ ARLETTY ▪ PATRICK BARR ▪ RICHARD BEYMER ▪ BOURVIL ▪ RICHARD BURTON ▪ RED BUTTONS ▪ SEAN CONNER
AN ▪ MEL FERRER ▪ HENRY FONDA ▪ STEVE FORREST ▪ GERT FROBE ▪ LEO GENN ▪ JOHN GREGSON ▪ DONALD HOUSTON
PETER LAWFORD ▪ CHRISTIAN MARQUAND ▪ RODDY McDOWALL
OBERT MITCHUM ▪ KENNETH MORE ▪ EDMOND O'BRIEN ▪ LESLIE PHILLIPS
N ▪ ROBERT RYAN ▪ TOMMY SANDS ▪ ROD STEIGER ▪ RICHARD TODD
YCK ▪ ROBERT WAGNER ▪ STUART WHITMAN ▪ JOHN WAYNE

The assault on Omaha Beach recreated in *The Longest Day*. Extras playing US soldiers did not want to jump into the sea from their landing craft until the film star Robert Mitchum led the way.

of Free French soldiers as they swarm along a harbour towards a German position on top of the casino at Ouistreham. The epic action is punctuated by a touching moment when French nuns brave the fighting to help the wounded. Another epic scene shows the US Rangers storming German gun emplacements on the cliffs at Pointe du Hoc.

Some of the actors had served in World War II. Richard Todd, who plays glider commander John Howard in the film, actually took part in the aerial assault on Pegasus Bridge as a paratrooper in 1944. Several veterans of D-Day also served as military consultants on the film, including John Howard who had led Richard Todd two decades earlier on the day

of the action. In the film, Todd jokes that the Paras are late, referring to his role as part of the paratrooper reinforcements sent in after the main glider attack. In a further layer of reality, another actor played the role of the real paratrooper Todd.

Despite the enormous cost of the movie – at $10 million the most expensive black and white film up to that time – it eventually became a box-office success.

In *The Longest Day*, John Wayne (right) plays 82nd Airborne officer Lieutenant Colonel Benjamin Vandervoot, who led his men into action despite a broken ankle.

THE GREAT ESCAPE

Date: **1963** Duration: **172 min**

Director:

John Sturges

Writers:

James Clavell, W R Burnett

A poster for *The Great Escape*, a film based on the mass escape of British Commonwealth prisoners from the German POW camp Stalag Luft III in 1944, in modern-day Poland.

Richard **ATTENBOROUGH**

COLOUR BY DE LUXE
PANAVISION®

ESCAPE

Produced &
Directed by JOHN
STURGES · Screenplay by JAMES **CLAVELL & BURNETT** · W.R. Based upon the book by PAUL **BRICKHILL**

Music by ELMER **BERNSTEIN** A MIRISCH-ALPHA PICTURE UNITED ARTISTS

A perennial favourite prisoner of war escape movie, its theme tune is still heard on football terraces during England games – especially when they're playing Germany. The story is based on the true mass escape from German POW camp Stalag Luft III in 1944 in Sagan, now located in Poland, and some of the characters are based on real wartime prisoners, but the American dimension is largely fictional. Or, as Wing Commander Ken Rees, long said to be the model for the Steve McQueen character puts it: 'It's always said that he was based on me, apart from him being a 6ft-tall American and me a Welshman of about 4ft 3in who can't ride a motorbike.'

The story begins with a mix of Allied prisoners assembled in a maximum security camp designed to frustrate those accused of regular escape attempts from other camps. 'There will be no escapes from this camp,' barks the German commandant. Chief among the previous failed escapers is RAF Squadron Leader Bartlett, played by Richard Attenborough, and he immediately sets about organising the digging of three tunnels for a mass break-out. An ensemble of top actors includes Donald Pleasence as the camp forger who nearly goes blind and James Coburn as an ingenious Australian devising ways to ventilate the tunnels. A clash of personalities is provided by Steve McQueen,

playing the rebellious USAAF Captain Hilts – the 'Cooler King' – who wants to build a shorter tunnel exiting just beyond the edge of the camp. Several failures and tunnel collapses build the tension towards the night of the final escape. There are many iconic scenes, including the moment when McQueen, riding a motorbike, tries to jump over a barbed wire fence.

The screenplay was based on the non-fiction book of the same name by Paul Brickhill, who had been imprisoned in the German camp, but much of the storyline is fictional with characters devised to fit around international stars. It was Steve McQueen, a keen biker, who insisted on the motorcycle scene. Of all the top stars, Donald Pleasence was the only one who had actually served a year in a German camp, after being shot down as an RAF pilot. The film was shot in Bavaria where the entire camp was constructed. It was a big box-office success and continues to be shown regularly on TV to this very day.

Steve McQueen on the famous TT Special 650 Triumph motorcycle in a publicity still for *The Great Escape*. McQueen's skill in riding a motorcycle meant he also played the German soldiers chasing him during his escape; however, the jump scene in which McQueen launches his motorcycle over barbed wire was actually performed by a stunt double.

RIGHT Director John Sturges and actors Richard Attenborough and James Garner on the set of *The Great Escape*. Most of the film was shot in Bavaria and a replica of Stalag Luft III was constructed in a large clearing within the Perlacher forest.

Film number: **19**

633 SQUADRON

Date: **1964**   Duration: **102 min**
Director:
Walter Grauman
Writers:
James Clavell, Howard Koch

Actor Cliff Robertson (left) as Wing Commander Roy Grant. Robertson was in fact an experienced pilot and collector of World War II era aircraft, owning several models including a genuine Supermarine Spitfire. His experience as a pilot was a major factor in his getting the part and adds an element of authenticity to the film.

Celebrating the exploits of Mosquito aerial raiders, this film follows a mission conducted by a fictional RAF squadron in World War II. The de Havilland Mosquito was a wood-constructed fast bomber – in 1941, one of the fastest aircraft in the world – and was used in several daring daytime raids on Nazi headquarters. The idea of these to launch pinpoint strikes at key operational targets and thus raise the morale of resistance fighters in occupied Europe.

In *633 Squadron*, the target is a Norwegian factory producing fuel for Hitler's V-2 rockets. As it is sited in a narrow fjord guarded by anti-aircraft guns, the aircraft will need to shatter the cliff that overhangs the fuel plant. As in the real raids, it is organised in conjunction with a local resistance group, who, in this case, promise to neutralise the batteries of guns. As the pilots practise for the raid in Scotland, the leader of the Norwegian resistance is captured and tortured by the Nazis. In an echo of a real

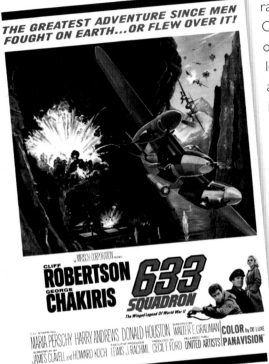

A poster for *633 Squadron*, a film inspired by the daytime raids on key Nazi installations conducted by RAF Mosquito pilots during World War II.

raid against Gestapo headquarters in Copenhagen in 1945, a single aircraft of the fictional 633 Squadron flies in low to destroy the Gestapo building and kill the Norwegian resistance leader. With the local resistance unable to destroy the anti-aircraft guns protecting the V-2 fuel plant, the pilots of 633 Squadron have to decide whether they will still take on the now suicidal task.

The film was based on a novel by Frederick E Smith inspired by the real Mosquito raids of World War II. Best-selling author James Clavell co-wrote the script. Its original hero was British, but in order to attract a wider world audience, the American star Cliff Robertson took the role. He was, however, an experienced pilot and would later buy his own Spitfire, so bringing a degree of authenticity to the part. This was further enhanced by the director, a veteran B-25 bomber pilot and a collector of vintage aircraft, using eight wartime Mosquito bombers in most of the action scenes. For many aircraft enthusiasts, this makes the film a must-watch classic. Filmed in the Scottish Highlands, the region's numerous lochs stood in for the Norwegian fjord, and George Lucas is said to have been inspired by the final low-flying fjord hugging scene of the film when he came to direct Luke Skywalker's aerial assault on the Death Star in *Star Wars Episode IV: A New Hope*.

George Chakiris (left), Maria Perschy (centre) and Cliff Robertson (right) in a publicity still for the film *633 Squadron*. The fictional RAF Sutton Craddock bomber airfield seen here is in fact RAF Bovingdon, Hertfordshire which, although officially closed in 1968, has since featured in a host of international films and television series.

Film number: **20**

VON RYAN'S EXPRESS

Date: **1965**   Duration: **158 min**

Director:

Mark Robson

Writers:

Wendell Mayes, Joseph Landon

Frank Sinatra as US Army Air Corps pilot Colonel Joseph Ryan, who is shot down and imprisoned in an Italian POW camp, along with other British soldiers. Although initially unpopular with his fellow prisoners Ryan soon earns their respect by confronting the camp's commandant, an act that sees him thrown in the 'sweat box'.

Frank Sinatra enjoyed a much-needed popular success with this World War II adventure, playing a prisoner of war leading an escape on a train from a prison camp in Italy. Much of the initial drama stems from the clash of personalities between Sinatra as US Army Air Corps Colonel Ryan and British Major Fincham, played by Trevor Howard. Immediately, Ryan annoys the mainly British prisoners by assuming command because he is the senior ranking officer. He also pursues a different approach to the camp commandant, Major Battaglia, by informing on the British attempts to escape by tunnel. But Ryan begins to earn their respect when he stands up to the commandant and ends up being imprisoned in a cramped metal 'sweat box'.

A poster for *Von Ryan's Express*. The film was based on the best-selling book by David Westheimer, who had been a POW during World War II, and of which Frank Sinatra was a big fan. Upon hearing that 20th Century Fox had purchased the film rights for a substantial sum, Sinatra immediately applied for the lead role.

A scene showing Sinatra's men as they make their daring escape, hiding atop the train as it rattles through the picturesque mountains of Italy.

When the war ends for Italy, the guards flee the camp and Ryan again flies in the face of British demands for vengeance by sparing Battaglia the death penalty, settling for punishing him by putting him in the 'sweat box'. The prisoners then break out across the Italian landscape, but the Germans, who now occupy the country, hunt them down, killing many of them, thanks to Battaglia's help. Fincham is furious that Ryan's leniency has cost the lives of his men. 'You'll get your Iron Cross now, *von* Ryan!' he says. The rest of the film is an exciting and suspenseful thriller as the surviving prisoners of war use an express train to escape from the Germans.

The film was based on a novel by David Westheimer, who had been a prisoner of war in Germany, but altered many aspects of it. Sinatra had liked it so much he wanted to buy the rights to the book himself and continued to have a major influence on the film, including changing the ending. He also changed the character of Ryan, making him more in tune with his own more relaxed West Coast style, or as one New York reviewer put it at the time: 'From here on it's the top rat of the Rat Pack leading the shoot-'em-up boys on their freedom run.' The film was shot in Italy, making the most of the locomotive rattling through spectacular locations, with an especially atmospheric scene set among ancient Roman ruins.

Film number: **21**

THE DIRTY DOZEN

Date: **1967**   Duration: **150 min**
Director:
Robert Aldrich
Writers:
Lukas Heller, Nunnally Johnson

A pulp fiction-style poster for *The Dirty Dozen*. A huge commercial success, the film inspired later directors like Quentin Tarantino.

The Dirty Dozen pose for a publicity shot, including Telly Savalas (kneeling left), Jim Brown (standing behind him with leg bent), Donald Sutherland (crouching with gun).

A great set-up for an action movie with an impressive cast to match, *The Dirty Dozen* begins with a US Army major, played by Lee Marvin, tasked with recruiting a commando unit for a virtual suicide mission against senior German army officers based in a chateau in Nazi occupied France, just prior to D-Day in 1944. For the operation, he recruits a dozen military prisoners facing execution or long sentences for their crimes. They include Charles Bronson, a German-speaking Polish American who attacked a superior officer, Telly Savalas, a woman-hating psychopath, John Cassavetes, an Italian American gangster, a slow-witted Donald Sutherland and Jim Brown, an African American who killed a man in self-defence.

At first reluctant to respond to discipline, various punishments bring them into line, including depriving them of water for shaving, hence the name 'Dirty Dozen'. But of course, it's the unconventional, rebellious nature of their characters that is the real 'dirt' and very much part of a 1960s movie-making mood playing

Lee Marvin and members of the Dirty Dozen attack senior German army officers based in a French chateau at the climax of the movie. Most of the filming was completed in England, and the chateau was constructed especially for the production.

with the traditional war movie genre. After training, they parachute into France, but their criminal flaws immediately get them into trouble when Savalas sadistically attacks a woman, alerting the Germans. Graphic violence follows as the men wreak havoc on the Nazis.

The film was based on a novel by E M Nathanson, which in turn was inspired by the true story of the 'Filthy Thirteen', a demolition unit of the 506th Parachute Infantry Regiment. Assigned missions behind enemy lines in 1944, half of them did not return. A celebrated photograph at the time showed two of them with Mohawk haircuts applying war-paint to each other. 'We weren't murderers or anything,' said one of their members, 'we just didn't do everything we were supposed to do in some ways and did a whole lot more than they wanted us to do in other ways. We were always in trouble.'

The 'punk' sensibility of the film influenced directors like Quentin Tarantino, who later commented 'You can't make a movie like *The Dirty Dozen* today. Actors like Ernest Borgnine and Charles Bronson were real men! Some of the men in acting back then went to war. Today's young actors are SOFT.' That was certainly true of Charles Bronson who served as a nose-gunner in a B-29 on 26 bombing missions against the Japanese and received a Purple Heart for wounds in combat.

Film number: **22**

WHERE EAGLES DARE

Date: **1968**   Duration: **158 min**

Director:

Brian G Hutton

Writer:

Alistair MacLean

A poster for *Where Eagles Dare*, a World War II action-adventure film in which a small team of Allied soldiers are sent to rescue US Army Brigadier General George Carnaby (Robert Beatty) after he is captured and taken to castle Adler, high in the Bavarian Alps, for interrogation.

Metro-Goldwyn-Mayer presents
...rry Gershwin-Elliott Kastner picture
starring

RICHARD BURTON
CLINT EASTWOOD

MARY URE

PATRICK WYMARK · MICHAEL HORDERN

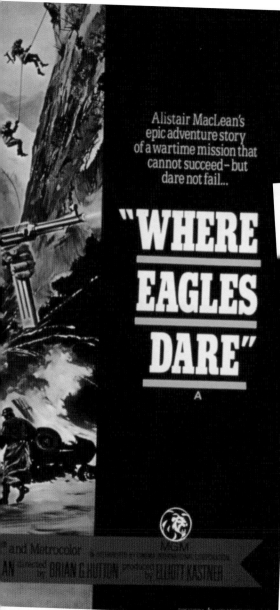

Alistair MacLean's
epic adventure story
of a wartime mission that
cannot succeed – but
dare not fail...

"WHERE
EAGLES
DARE"

A

A British adventure film set in World War II, *Where Eagles Dare* follows a mission to rescue an American general held in a mountaintop fortress and is notable for its action sequences featuring top Hollywood actors Richard Burton and Clint Eastwood. Burton plays Major Smith, leading British commandos, and Eastwood is US Army Ranger Lieutenant Schaffer.

Clint Eastwood poses with a German MP40 in a publicity still for *Where Eagles Dare*. Eastwood's quiet demeanor was well suited for the role of Lieutenant Schaffer who is at the epicenter of most action scenes.

Parachuted into the Bavarian Alps, Smith, Schaffer and their team are clad in German uniforms as they advance towards the fortress, but all is not as it seems and the true mission is revealed to be about exposing enemy Nazi agents. Said the movie tagline: 'They look like Nazis but… The Major is British… The Lieutenant is American… The Beautiful Frauleins are Allied Agents!' The convolutions of the plot are balanced by exciting action scenes including a celebrated fight on top of a cable car. Some of these sequences involved special effects, such as front projection, one of the first uses of this new method of combining foreground action with a pre-filmed background landscape. So many stuntmen were required that it was dubbed 'Where Doubles Dare.' Thriller writer Alistair MacLean created the story especially for the film, following his trademark secret traitor storylines. The striking title comes from a line in Shakespeare's *Richard III*: 'The world is grown so bad, that wrens make prey where eagles dare not perch.'

Eastwood thought the script was too exposition heavy and asked for less dialogue and more action, but it was a useful transition for him from the 'spaghetti western' movies that had made his name. 'My agent

felt it would be a great idea to pair up with an actor senior to me,' he recalled. 'Richard was quite a character and of course he was with Miss Taylor at the time, they were sort of the couple. I was the young guy who didn't have to worry too much.' For Burton it was a much-needed box-office hit and he mentioned *The Guns of Navarone* to the producer as the type of adventure movie he wanted to star in. This was based on a MacLean book and sparked the author's involvement in the film, becoming his first screenplay, which was then turned into a novel. The film was shot in Austria and Bavaria, and castle Hohenwerfen's location high above the medieval town of Werfen is still a popular tourist sight today.

The famous cable car scene in *Where Eagles Dare*. The film employed so many stunt doubles it was dubbed 'Where Doubles Dare'. The famous 1960s stuntman Alf Joint lost numerous teeth during this particular sequence, when he jumped to the cable car's roof.

Film number: **23**

HELL IN THE PACIFIC

Date: **1969**   Duration: **102 min**

Director:

John Boorman

Writers:

Alexander Jacobs, Eric Bercovici

Two opposing soldiers, played by Lee Marvin and Toshiro Mifune, are stranded on a Pacific island in World War II and battle to survive in *Hell in the Pacific*.

Just two men stranded on an island in the middle of the Pacific, one is a US Marine pilot, the other a Japanese naval officer. When they realise they are not alone, they pursue their own private war against each other. They steal each other's salvaged equipment, compete over drinking water and fight each other.

At one point, the Japanese makes the Marine his prisoner, yoking him with a branch from a tree, but the officer has no taste for this cruelty and is relieved when the American escapes. Then the American captures the Japanese, harnessing him to the same

Out of violence, compassion.
Out of suspicion, trust.
Out of hell, hope.

LEE
MARVIN

TOSHIRO
MIFUNE

:ELMUR PICTURES and HENRY G. SAPERSTEIN present **HELL
IN THE
PACIFIC**

LALO SCHIFRIN · ALEXANDER JACOBS · ERIC BERCOVICI · REUBEN BERCOVITCH
HENRY G. SAPERSTEIN · SELIG J. SELIGMAN · REUBEN BERCOVITCH · JOHN BOORMAN
PANAVISION · TECHNICOLOR

yoke hauling driftwood, but the American gets as little satisfaction from the reversal as did his captor, and he cuts the man free. Then, in the face of their shared need to survive, they forge an unspoken truce. They fish together and build a raft. There is very little dialogue, and the two men struggle to understand each other. A lack of subtitles means the audience shares their frustration.

Robinson Crusoe in a war setting, *Hell in the Pacific* was produced by Reuben Bercovitch from his original story and elevated by inspired casting. Toshiro Mifune, playing the Japanese officer, had taken the lead in several great Akira Kurosawa samurai films,

A poster for *Hell in the Pacific* featuring the two great actors, Lee Marvin and Toshiro Mifune. Both men served in World War II for their respective countries, Marvin in the US Marine Corps and Mifune in the Imperial Japanese Army Air Service.

including *Rashomon*, *Seven Samurai* and *Throne of Blood*. Lee Marvin was the American tough guy star of *The Professionals*, *The Dirty Dozen* and *Point Blank*. Both men had served their country in their respective armed forces during the war in the Pacific. Marvin was a Marine and took part in the battle of Saipan where he was wounded and received the Purple Heart. Mifune was in the Imperial Japanese Army Air Service.

The entire production was filmed on five of the Palau Islands of Micronesia. Director John Boorman (who had also directed Marvin in *Point Blank*) wanted a location that would be savage as well as beautiful – a theme of survival in the wilderness that would be revisited in his brilliant *Deliverance* in 1972. *Hell in the Pacific* was not a commercial success and thanks to its expensive set locations lost money, but the virtuoso performances of the two lead actors make it a gripping wartime tale. The original ending was rather abrupt, underlining the futility of their struggle, but an alternative ending was added to the DVD release of the film in 2004.

After subjecting one another to torture the two men forge an unspoken truce as they soon learn that in order to escape their island prison they must work together.

Film number: **24**

BATTLE OF BRITAIN

Date: **1969**   Duration: **133 min**
Director:
Guy Hamilton
Writers:
James Kennaway, Wilfred Greatorex

A large number of period aircraft was needed for the film, not just Spitfires but also German Heinkel bombers and many more models from the 1940s. In total, over 100 vintage aircraft were used for the aerial sequences.

A brilliant recreation of the aerial campaign over Britain in 1940, *Battle of Britain* is notable for both its excellent script and superb air combat scenes. It really is a great example of a film as national war memorial, celebrating an enormous military achievement against the odds and yet not shying away from portraying the individual sacrifice that made victory possible.

The film begins during the dismal days of Dunkirk, echoing the words of British wartime leader Winston Churchill that the battle of France was over and the battle of Britain was about to begin. We see one Spitfire pilot ill-advisedly giving a victory roll over retreating columns of British soldiers and French refugees, hoping to raise their morale, he claims, but underlining the RAF's inability to stop the German blitzkrieg. We then hear the words of Air Chief Marshal Hugh Dowding, played by leading English actor Laurence Olivier, explaining that there is no point risking their precious aircraft in futile gestures in France and that the aircraft must be preserved for the defence of Britain.

The history is told with greater wit and economy than in previous

"**Battle of Britain**"

A poster for *Battle of Britain*, a film inspired by the Royal Air Force and its defence of Britain against the German Luftwaffe's campaign of attack, which began in June 1940. Continually frustrated by the RAF Hitler eventually abandoned his invasion plans, codenamed Operation Sea Lion, though the bombing of London continued throughout the war's duration.

A young Michael Caine as Squadron Leader Canfield. Alongside Caine the film's star-studded cast featured such names as Laurence Olivier and Trevor Howard.

epic movies such as *The Longest Day*, which seems a little ponderous in comparison. The film is full of great one-liners, especially when German Luftwaffe commander Hermann Göring is berating his officers for their failure. He then lightens his tone, instead asking what he can do for them to help. 'Give me a squadron of Spitfires,' says one of them dryly. The script is based on the book *The Narrow Margin* by Derek Wood and Derek Dempster and deftly follows the stages of the battle from near annihilation of the RAF to merciful relief when German bombers are order to attack London instead. The film climaxes with the RAF victorious in the air battle of 15 September 1940.

To capture the aerial fight sequences 100 vintage aircraft were assembled, and later models of the Spitfires were adapted to look like those of 1940. Many of the German Heinkel bombers were later Spanish-built versions, as were the Messerschmitt fighters, all of which were altered to look like the original aircraft. The use of real aircraft, rather than models, gives the combat scenes an authenticity that makes them impressive, even in today's digital age of special effects. Renowned German fighter ace Adolf Galland was one of several World War II veterans who acted as advisers on the film set.

OH! WHAT A LOVELY WAR

Date: **1969** Duration: **144 min**
Director:
Richard Attenborough
Writer:
Len Deighton

A poster for *Oh! What a Lovely War* with the tag-line 'The ever popular war game with songs battles & a few jokes' highlighting the film's satirical nature.

A dazzling directorial debut from Richard Attenborough that for some is a superb anti-war satire, but for others is an over-egged melange of World War I clichés. Based on the 1963 stage musical of the same name by Joan Littlewood and her Theatre Workshop, and a radio play by Charles Chilton, it uses music-hall songs to depict the absurdity of the Great War and its terrible losses.

The stage show was inspired in part by *The Donkeys*, itself a flawed critique of World War I generals by Alan Clark, part of a 1960s mood of anti-Establishment historical criticism that produced an updated version of *The Charge of the Light Brigade* in 1968 that also satirised the errors of British commanders. Many leading academics now question this vision of the Great War as a pointless conflict made worse by bungling generals, but it remains an enormously popular interpretation and *Oh! What a Lovely War* continued to resonate in more recent productions such as the BBC TV comedy *Blackadder Goes Forth*.

The film begins on Brighton West Pier with actors representing the leaders of Europe walking over a map of the continent as events draw them towards war. The German Kaiser and Russian Czar are compromised by their army mobilisation timetables in a portrayal of

THE EVER POPULAR WAR GAME WITH SONGS BATTLES & A FEW JOKES

Paramount Pictures presents
An Accord Production

Oh! What a Lovely War

DIRK BOGARDE
PHYLLIS CALVERT
JEAN PIERRE CASSEL
JOHN CLEMENTS
JOHN GIELGUD
JACK HAWKINS
KENNETH MORE

LAURENCE OLIVIER
MICHAEL REDGRAVE
VANESSA REDGRAVE
RALPH RICHARDSON
MAGGIE SMITH
SUSANNAH YORK
JOHN MILLS as Sir Douglas Haig

Produced by **Brian Duffy** and **Richard Attenborough**
Directed by **Richard Attenborough** Colour Panavision

the causes of war that shares the blame among all the old Establishment figures. We then follow the Smith family as their sons become soldiers on the Western Front. Maggie Smith plays an alluring music-hall singer willing to walk out every day with a new recruit if they take the King's Shilling, but as the young men take up her offer, she is shown in close-up as an old tart. British generals are mocked in a scene showing them leapfrogging over each other. As the war progresses, the mood and the accompanying songs become darker, including a rendition of 'Hanging on the Old Barbed Wire'. Poppies are used throughout the film as symbols of blood and death.

Although intellectually wanting, the final scenes of the film pack a mighty emotional punch. While the Smith family has a picnic, the spirits of dead soldiers settle on a beautiful Sussex hillside with their friends as the camera pulls back on an aerial shot of thousands of white crosses. It cannot fail to bring tears to your eyes.

Sir Edward Grey (Ralph Richardson), Kaiser Wilhelm II (Kenneth More), Count Leopold Berchtold (John Gielgud) and other heads of state in a scene from *Oh! What a Lovely War*.

Guest star John Mills as General Sir Douglas Haig. The iconic image of Haig standing amongst thousands of white crosses is poignant to say the least. He was the commander of the British Expeditionary Force on the Western Front in World War I.

Film number: **26**

M*A*S*H

Date: **1970**   Duration: **116 min**
Director:
Robert Altman
Writer:
Ring Lardner Jr
Academy Award:
For best adapted screenplay

A poster for the 1970 comedy M*A*S*H.

About a Mobile Army Surgical Hospital in the Korean War, M*A*S*H was an enormously successful war comedy that spawned an equally popular TV series. Its irreverent take on the US Army and an Asian conflict was perfect for the times and gave a lighter note to the political angst associated with the Vietnam War. Altman wanted the Vietnam reference to be stronger, but the studio 20th Century Fox underlined its Korean setting by mentioning it in the opening sequence. The director was a veteran of World War II, having served as a B24 pilot, and wanted the hospital operating scenes to be authentic and bloody.

Donald Sutherland, who played a hippy-style tanker in Kelly's Heroes, released in the same year, was the perfect anti-hero actor for the role of Captain 'Hawkeye' Pierce, while Elliot Gould took on Captain 'Trapper John' McIntyre. Both are chaotic women-chasing rebels who also happen to be excellent military surgeons, but their laid-back style causes clashes with a rival surgeon and the unit's chief nurse, Major O'Houlihan, played by Sally Kellerman.

When Hawkeye and Trapper mischievously broadcast O'Houlihan having sex with a religiously minded colleague, she earns the camp nickname of 'Hot Lips'. 'This isn't a hospital!' she famously complains to her commanding officer.

20th Century-Fox presents

M*A*S*H

An Ingo Preminger Production

Starring

DONALD SUTHERLAND · ELLIOTT GOULD
TOM SKERRITT

Co-Starring
SALLY KELLERMAN · ROBERT DUVALL · JO ANN PFLUG · RENE AUBERJONOIS

Produced by INGO PREMINGER · Directed by ROBERT ALTMAN

Screenplay by RING LARDNER, Jr.

From a novel by RICHARD HOOKER · Music by JOHNNY MANDEL

PANAVISION* · COLOUR by DE LUXE®

Donald Sutherland (left) and Elliot Gould (right) as Captain Benjamin 'Hawkeye' Pierce and Captain 'Trapper John' McIntyre, two gifted army surgeons with a lust for women and a rebellious nature.

'It's an insane asylum, and it's your fault!' Further farcical incidents involve a dentist convinced he is homosexual and O'Houlihan being exposed while having a shower. The film very much promotes the liberal values of California at the time against stern military discipline and now seems dated in its attitudes towards homosexuality and women.

The script was based on a novel by Richard Hooker and critics loved its subversive tone. It was the first major film to include an expletive 'f**k' in its script, although this was taken out for later television screenings. Thanks to its box office success, it was developed into a long-running TV series. The TV title sequence featured the music from the theme song of the original film, 'Suicide is Painless,' the lyrics to which were written by Mike Altman, son of the director. As a result the younger Altman earned more from song royalties than his father did from directing the film. The helicopters used in the drama were authentic Bell 47s, designated H-13 Sioux helicopters in the army.

One of the most memorable scenes in *M*A*S*H*, the football game between the two rival units of the 4077th Mobile Army Surgical Hospital.

Film number: **27**

PATTON: LUST FOR GLORY

Date: **1970**   Duration: **171 min**

Director:

Franklin J Schaffner

Writers:

Francis Ford Coppola &
Edmund H North

Academy Awards:

For best picture, director, screenplay, actor (George C Scott), art
direction, editing, and sound

The drama of this film comes from the central character study and clash of two contrasting US generals in World War II, George C Scott brilliantly playing the charismatic but headstrong General George S Patton and Karl Malden performing the more thoughtful and professional role of General Omar N Bradley.

The notorious scene in *Patton: Lust for Glory*, when the general strikes a soldier suffering from shell shock. Patton was subsequently removed from command.

"THE EPIC AMERICAN WAR MOVIE THAT HOLLYWOOD HAS ALWAYS WANTED TO MAKE BUT NEVER HAD THE GUTS TO DO BEFORE."
—Vincent Canby, New York Times

OU MAY NEVER HAVE ANOTHER XPERIENCE LIKE IT! EVIDENTLY MEONE BELIEVED THAT THE PUBLIC D COME OF AGE ENOUGH TO KE A MATURE FILM ABOUT A L WAR WITH A HERO-VILLAIN LL HIS GLORIOUS AND NGLORIOUS HUMANITY."
—Liz Smith, Cosmopolitan Magazine

PATTON

GEORGE C. SCOTT / KARL MALDEN in "PATTON"

Patton reinvigorates American forces in North Africa following their crushing defeat by the Germans at the Kasserine Pass, but then comes a cropper in Sicily when he slaps a soldier suffering from shell shock during a hospital visit – a scene vividly recreated in the film. The headline-making scandal following this sees Patton relieved of his command and sent back to Britain. The Germans, however, cannot believe that the one American commander they respect has been removed over what they consider a trivial incident and are convinced he has been moved to head a major assault on Europe. And indeed Patton becomes part of the Allied campaign of misinformation to hide the true landing location.

Publicity material for *Patton: Lust for Glory*, released in 1970. The promotion for the film focused on the general's larger than life, swaggering personality.

George C Scott plays General Patton during a recreation of the US Seventh Army landing in Sicily in 1943 for *Patton: Lust for Glory*.

The screenplay, co-written by a young Francis Ford Coppola, is full of unusual moments. The famous opening scene shows Patton in front of an enormous Stars and Stripes flag delivering a strident speech full of expletives. 'Now, I want you to remember that no bastard ever won a war by dying for his country,' says Scott as Patton. 'He won it by making the other poor dumb bastard die for his country.' On another occasion, in North Africa, Patton visits the ancient battlefield of Zama and tells Bradley that he believes he was there in a former life.

'The script was very controversial when I wrote it, because they thought it was so stylised,' recalled Coppola. 'I had this very bizarre opening where he stands up in front of an American flag and gives this speech [but] ultimately the stuff that I got in trouble for, the casting for *The Godfather* or the flag scene in *Patton*, was the stuff that was remembered, and was considered really the good work.' The powerful script combined with Scott's swaggering performance and spectacular battlefield scenes, deploying the Spanish Army as extras, ensured it won seven Oscars in 1971, including one for best picture. Scott declined to accept his for best actor – the first actor ever to do so.

Film number: **28**

TORA! TORA! TORA!

Date: **1970**   Duration: **144 min**

Director:

Richard Fleischer

Writer:

Larry Forrester

Academy Award:

For best special visual effects

UK publicity material for the
video release of *Tora! Tora! Tora!*

TORA! TORA! TORA!

**For the first time
once-warring nations combine
to tell their true story of
Pearl Harbour...
History's greatest air-sea battle.**

20th Century Fox presents   **TORA! TORA! TORA!** u   AN ELMO WILLIAMS
For the United States Sequences: For the Japanese Sequences: RICHARD FLEISCHER PRODUCTION
Starring MARTIN BALSAM as "Admiral Kimmel"   Starring SOH YAMAMURA as "Admiral Yamamoto"
JOSEPH COTTEN as "Henry L Stimson"   E G MARSHALL as "Lt Col Kramer"   TATSUYA MIHASHI as "Cdr Genda"   TAKAHIRO TAMURA as "Lt Cdr Fuchida"
JAMES WHITMORE as "Admiral William F Halsey"   EIJIRO TONO as "Adm Nagumo"   KOREYA SENDA as "Prince Konoye"
AND JASON ROBARDS as "General Short"   Assoc Producer OTTO LANG   Directed by TORUO MASUDA and KINJI FUKASAKU
Screenplay by LARRY FORRESTER, HIDEO OGUNI and RYUZO KIKUSHIMA
Music by JERRY GOLDSMITH   Produced by ELMO WILLIAMS   Directed by RICHARD FLEISCHER
PANAVISION® COLOUR BY DE LUXE

Pearl Harbor – the Japanese pre-emptive strike that thrust the United States into World War II – has been surprisingly poorly served by American feature film depictions, many of which fail to deliver satisfying drama, but *Tora! Tora! Tora!* is one of the more successful versions, partly because it shows the war triggering events from the view of the Japanese as well as the Americans.

After his success with *The Longest Day*, producer Daryl F Zanuck wanted to make an epic movie about Pearl Harbor that had a similar multi-perspective, Cornelius Ryan-style narrative of the event, seeing it from both sides. By doing this, he hoped to correct the impression that American failure was wholly to blame as the film would depict the brilliance of the Japanese operation as well. Indeed, the film took its title from the Japanese codeword for 'lightning attack', signifying its success, although its literal meaning is 'tiger'. To achieve this dual perspective the film was shot as two separate productions in the US and Japan.

Akira Kurosawa was originally hired to direct and write the Japanese storyline, but he was replaced during shooting by two other more malleable Japanese directors. 'I felt he was not only uncomfortable directing this

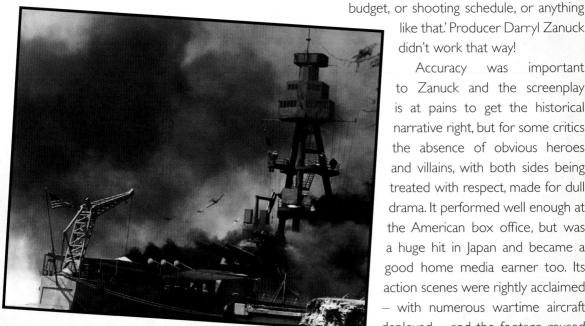

Japanese planes bomb US battleships anchored at Pearl Harbor for the recreation of the notorious attack in *Tora! Tora! Tora!*

kind of movie,' noted Fleischer about the legendary Japanese film director, 'but also he wasn't used to having somebody tell him how he should make his film. He always had complete autonomy, and nobody would dare make a suggestion to Kurosawa about the budget, or shooting schedule, or anything like that.' Producer Darryl Zanuck didn't work that way!

Accuracy was important to Zanuck and the screenplay is at pains to get the historical narrative right, but for some critics the absence of obvious heroes and villains, with both sides being treated with respect, made for dull drama. It performed well enough at the American box office, but was a huge hit in Japan and became a good home media earner too. Its action scenes were rightly acclaimed – with numerous wartime aircraft deployed – and the footage reused in subsequent war movies, although US post-war aircraft carriers had to stand in for Japanese vessels. Minoru Genda, the Japanese naval officer and pilot who helped devise the aerial raid, was both portrayed in the film and an uncredited technical adviser for it.

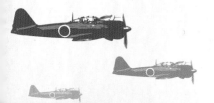

Japanese pilots celebrate their successful raid on Pearl Harbor in a recreated scene.

Film number: **29**

A BRIDGE TOO FAR

Date: **1977** Duration: **176 min**
Director:
Richard Attenborough
Writer:
William Goldman

The original poster for *A Bridge Too Far* highlighting the film's ensemble cast of A-list actors which included Sean Connery, Michael Caine, Robert Redford, Gene Hackman, Laurence Olivier and many more.

OUT OF THE SKY COMES THE SCREEN'S MOST INCREDIBLE SPECTACLE OF MEN AND WAR!

Joseph E. Levine presents
A BRIDGE TOO FAR
starring (in alphabetical order)
Dirk Bogarde
James Caan
Michael Caine
Sean Connery
Edward Fox
Elliott Gould
Gene Hackman
Anthony Hopkins
Hardy Kruger
Laurence Olivier
Ryan O'Neal
Robert Redford
Maximilian Schell
Liv Ullmann
From the book by
Cornelius Ryan
Screenplay by
William Goldman
Produced by
Joseph E. Levine
and
Richard P. Levine
Directed by
Richard Attenborough
Music Composed and Conducted by
John Addison
Color United Artists
A Transamerica Company

Joseph E. Levine presents
A BRIDGE TOO FAR

Sean Connery (left) plays Major General Roy Urquhart, commander of the 1st Airborne Division during Operation Market-Garden, in *A Bridge Too Far*.

Another epic war film based on the panoramic writing of Cornelius Ryan, this time telling the story of the forlorn attempt to capture a key bridge from the Germans at Arnhem during the Allied aerial assault of Operation Market-Garden in 1944. As with *The Longest Day*, the narrative follows the events through the actions of numerous real military figures played by an impressive roster of top international actors.

The film begins by describing the politics behind the campaign and the desire to end the war quickly by getting to Berlin before the Russians. It was intended to be the largest aerial assault in history, landing Allied troops behind enemy lines to secure bridges for a rapid armoured advance. As the film shows, however, German resistance is stronger than anticipated and some of the British troops land too far from the bridge at Arnhem. British paratroopers led by Major General Roy Urquhart, played by Sean Connery, fight a desperate last stand among the ruins of the Dutch town. Less than a fifth of his troops manage to escape, with many soldiers sacrificing themselves to cover their retreat. Michael Caine plays the commander of a Guards armoured unit, Robert Redford a US parachute commander and Gene Hackman a Polish paratrooper leader. Hundreds of extras were dropped by parachute from a Dakota aircraft in a spectacular reconstruction of the attack. The fighting around the bridge was shot at a similar looking bridge in the Dutch town of Deventer.

The film explores the failure of Operation Market-Garden, the Allied plan to break through German lines in the Netherlands, seize numerous bridges of key strategic importance and outflank the German defences in an attempt to end the war by Christmas 1944.

In the film, the finger of blame for the operation's failure is pointed at Lieutenant General Frederick 'Boy' Browning, commander of the 1st Airborne Corps in north-west Europe, played by Dirk Bogarde. A film reviewer picked this up, saying of him 'I would not have trusted him to run a cocktail party.' The film blighted his reputation ever after, despite the efforts of his wife, novelist Daphne du Maurier, to argue his case with the film director. It was Browning, incidentally, who is said to have coined the phrase 'a bridge too far' when warning Field Marshal Montgomery of the operational difficulties.

The fact that the film ultimately records a military failure may explain why it was not a great box office success, but it did perform better in Europe than America and its starry cast continues to make it an interesting movie.

Film number: **30**

CROSS OF IRON

Date: **1977**   Duration: **132 min**

Director:

Sam Peckinpah

Writers:

Julius J Epstein, Walter Kelley, James Hamilton

A poster for the film *Cross of Iron*. The German medal the Iron Cross is clearly visible in the centre. Predominantly a military decoration, there were a number of instances where civilians were awarded the Iron Cross for performing military functions during World War II.

Noted more for his ultra-violent Westerns, director Peckinpah's savage style suited this story set on the Eastern Front in World War II. An Anglo-German co-production, it was based on the novel *The Willing Flesh* by Willi Heinrich, which follows a battle-hardened German unit in 1943 retreating from the Taman Peninsula in the Russian Caucasus. It pits Prussian idealism against the brutal reality of their desperate situation.

The tone of the film is set from the start when Sergeant Steiner, played by James Coburn, and his ragged German unit overrun a Russian outpost, stabbing the defenders to death. They capture a boy soldier and are ordered to shoot him by Captain Stransky, played by Maximilian Schell, an arrogant Prussian officer who has transferred from a soft posting in France to frontline service in Russia so he can win an Iron Cross and maintain his family honour. Steiner refuses to execute the boy and the conflict between the two is established – Steiner later releases the boy only to see him shot by his own side.

Stransky then falsely claims a military success as his own in order to be nominated for the Iron Cross. At the end of the film, as the two men are pinned down by Russian fire, Steiner hands Stransky a machine gun, telling him 'I'll show you where the Iron Crosses grow.' He laughs when Stransky's gun jams and we see the face of another

not fighting

Ross of Iron

F IRON x
Film

MAXIMILIAN SCHELL · JAMES MASON

ENTA BERGER in the part of EVA

track Recording on EMI Records - EMA 782

A SAM PECKINPAH film

Screenplay by JULIUS J. EPSTEIN and HERBERT ASMODI
Music composed and conducted by ERNEST GOLD
Produced by WOLF C. HARTWIG · Directed by SAM PECKINPAH
A Winitsky-Sellers / Rapid Film Production. · An Anglo-German Co-Production
technicolor© · Distributed by EMI Film Distributors Limited.

NOW AVAILABLE AS A CORGI PAPERBACK

boy soldier, just like the one killed earlier in the film. The character of Steiner is said to be based on a real German NCO, Johann Schwerdfeger, who received the Knight's Cross of the Iron Cross with Oak Leaves for service on the Eastern Front.

The film was shot in Communist Yugoslavia and benefited enormously from the availability of Soviet era armour. An exciting scene set around a factory shows real T-34 tanks crashing into the German position. The broken pipes and steel wire of the factory interior make for a striking setting as one of the monstrous Russian tanks smashes through its wall and is covered with bricks as it hunts down the Germans. The pulp fiction quality of the bloody violence was a major inspiration for Tarantino's own war film, *Inglourious Basterds*. It did not perform well at the US box office, but had greater success in Europe, especially in Germany where audiences appreciated the no-holds-barred depiction of fighting on the Eastern Front.

ABOVE James Coburn as Sergeant Rolf Steiner. Coburn's character is based on a German NCO who received the prestigious Knight's Cross with Oak Leaves. The addition of golden oak leaves symbolised the display of personal gallantry or distinguished service.

OPPOSITE Segeant Steiner briefs his men before an engagement with Russian forces in *Cross of Iron*.

THE DEER HUNTER

Date: **1978** Duration: **182 min**

Director:

Michael Cimino

Writer:

Deric Washburn

Academy Awards:

For best picture, director, supporting actor (Christopher Walken), film editing, and sound

Poster for *The Deer Hunter* drawing attention to the controversial Russian roulette scene in the film.

Robert De Niro's character suffers from his experience as a prisoner of war in *The Deer Hunter* and cannot settle easily on his return back home.

A film focusing on the impact of war on a home community, *The Deer Hunter* tells the story of five close friends played by Robert De Niro, Christopher Walken, John Savage, John Cazale and Chuck Aspegren, workers in a Pennsylvania steel mill who like to relax on deer-hunting expeditions. A wedding party heralds three of them going off to fight in the Vietnam War. Two years later, in North Vietnam, the three are united just as swarms of Viet Cong make them prisoners of war. The horrors of a Viet Cong prison camp scar them for life. In one of the most controversial sequences of the film, all three American prisoners are forced to play Russian roulette by their Viet Cong captors. This prompts them to escape.

Back home in Pennsylvania, De Niro, apparently the sole survivor of the group, cannot face the welcoming party. He and the girlfriend of one his comrades, played by Meryl Streep, try to establish a relationship, but each is aware that the Christopher Walken character should be there instead. Trying to get back in his old routine, De Niro agrees to go hunting with his old friends, who stayed behind, but as De Niro stalks the animal, he realises he can no longer kill the deer. This is then cut with a scene of his shocking prison camp experiences. De Niro goes back to Vietnam to bring back Walken.

America's troubled relationship with its Vietnam war veterans and how traumatised soldiers cope with returning home was very much a point of debate in the 1970s, a prevalent mood that this film caught perfectly, but over the decades since, this recurrent problem within US society has not worn well and is perhaps one of the main reasons why this film is not an enduring favourite. *First Blood* in 1982, the first Rambo film, dealt with the same subject in a popular action form and is still widely screened now. *The Deer Hunter*'s worthiness and first class performances by its lead ensemble ensured it won five Oscars, one for best film of 1979, but it now seems overlong and pretentious. Cimino's follow-up film, *Heaven's Gate*, was a critical and commercial flop. '*Heaven's Gate* fails so completely,' wrote a New York critic, 'you might suspect Mr Cimino sold his soul to the Devil to obtain the success of *The Deer Hunter*, and the Devil has just come around to collect.'

Having escaped captivity at the hands of the Viet Cong, Sergeant Michael 'Mike' Vronsky (Robert De Niro) and Corporal Nikanor 'Nick' Chevotarevich (Christopher Walken) desperately cling to a US helicopter as its crew attempt to transport the pair to safety.

APOCALYPSE NOW

Date: 1979   **Duration: 153 min**

Director:

Francis Ford Coppola

Writers:

John Milius, Francis Ford Coppola

Academy Award:

For best cinematography (Vittorio Storaro)

Martin Sheen plays Captain Willard searching for Colonel Kurtz in *Apocalypse Now*, a journey that takes him deeper into the hell of the Vietnam War.

Apocalypse Now is firmly established as one of the greatest war movies ever made and regularly appears in the top ten of viewers' polls of their favourite movies. The film began as a script by John Milius in 1969, loosely based on Joseph Conrad's short story *Heart of Darkness*. Milius' script tells the story of US Captain Willard being sent to locate and terminate Colonel Kurtz, a rogue Green Beret who has set himself up as chieftain of a tribal kingdom in the remote jungle of Vietnam. It is a clever twist on Conrad's story, originally set in the 1890s in which Kurtz ruthlessly runs an ivory collecting station in the Congo and is corrupted by the brutality around him. The film is an horrific analysis of colonialism, showing how a European can be tempted to exert superhuman power at a cost to himself and those around him. A similar tale of European colonial vanity that ends badly, but told with a

lighter satirical tone, is John Huston's 1975 movie *The Man Who Would Be King*, based on Rudyard Kipling's story.

In *Apocalypse Now*, Kurtz, played by Marlon Brando, is a brilliant Special Forces officer sent into the wilderness to recruit Montagnard native forces in the war against North Vietnamese Communism. At the start of the film, Kurtz goes native and cruelly rules his little jungle kingdom. It is up to Willard, played by Martin Sheen, to end this embarrassment to US covert warfare and so begins an epic journey along a river into a modern heart of darkness.

When director Francis Coppola took on the project in 1975, the Vietnam War had just ended in defeat and he believed Milius' script was too jingoistic. He took his inspiration from UK filmmaker Ken Russell and wanted to make a more surreal vision of the conflict. He wanted it to be a psychedelic trip into the nature of war and violence. 'I mean the war is essentially

A poster for *Apocalypse Now* showing Marlon Brando.

a Los Angeles export,' he claimed, 'like acid rock…' In one of its most startling sequences, Coppola illustrates the intrusion of Western pop culture into South-East Asia with the Rolling Stones blaring out from a patrol boat while a soldier water-skis behind it. But it is in the explicit depiction of US soldiers too stoned on marijuana and acid to fight in a besieged outpost that Coppola gives full vent to his vision of Vietnam as a psychedelic hell. *Apocalypse Now* is a brilliant piece of cinema but it is more about the perils of western colonialism than the Vietnam War.

The most famous scene in *Apocalypse Now* shows an attack by US Air Cavalry in which a formation of helicopters play Wagner's *Ride of the Valkyries* from loudspeakers as they swoop in to secure a Viet Cong beach position, all so that their soldiers will have somewhere to surf. It seems incredible but the scene is based

on authentic US tactics, from 1965 onwards, in which Bell UH-1 Huey helicopters were used in mass assaults on enemy positions. They would come in low at tremendous speed, firing machine guns and rockets, and then deliver troops to the ground. In *Apocalypse Now*, during the helicopter assault, one character, played by Frederic Forrest, discovers the wisdom of sitting on his helmet during the attack because only the pilots were protected by armour plate. Bullets easily punched holes in the aluminium fuselage. Some Hueys were equipped with loudspeaker systems to be used mainly for psychological warfare against the enemy.

Coppola employed several military advisers while making *Apocalypse Now*, including US Marine Corps Captain Doug Ryan who advised on special unit military tactics. The film was made in the Philippines where many US-made helicopters and other surplus military equipment were available. The recreated napalm attack used 1,200 gallons of gasoline in 90 seconds.

A still from the famous scene showing US Air Cavalry helicopters attacking Viet Cong positions in *Apocalypse Now*.

THE BIG RED ONE

Date: **1980**   Duration: **113 min**

Director:

Samuel Fuller

Writer:

Samuel Fuller

Publicity for *The Big Red One*, a film about the US 1st Infantry Division fighting in North Africa in World War II. Samuel Fuller, a veteran soldier who served with the real US 1st Infantry, drew upon his wartime experiences when directing the film.

A war film coming out of the personal wartime experience of its director and writer, *The Big Red One* follows a unit from the US 1st Infantry Division – *The Big Red One* from the red numeral '1' on its shoulder patch – as it fights its way from North Africa to Germany in World War II. The cruel irony and deadly errors of war are at the heart of the film and one startling scene shows the Americans landing on a beach in North Africa only to be shot at by a French general loyal to the pro-Nazi Vichy regime. Many men die on both sides before the French soldiers, loyal to the Free France government-in-exile, overpower their leader. Fuller was a veteran of the war and the 1st Infantry Division, receiving a Bronze Star, Silver Star and Purple Heart.

Lee Marvin, experienced in playing cynical military anti-heroes, takes on the role of Sergeant Possum and the opening scenes flash back to World War I when he knifes a surrendering German soldier, just to be told later that the Armistice had been called four hours before. This needless

LORIMAR PRÉSENTE   un fi
LEE MARVIN · MARK HAM
avec ROBERT CARRADINE · BOI
produit par GEN

death haunts him throughout the movie. Mark Hamill, fresh from his *Star Wars* success as Luke Skywalker, is well cast as young rifleman Griff, who early on doubts he can kill the enemy. He tells the Sergeant: 'I can't murder anybody.' 'We don't murder; we kill,' explains Marvin. 'It's the same thing,' says Hamill. 'The hell it is, Griff,' counters the Sergeant. 'You don't murder animals; you kill 'em.'

Many of the beach scenes that feature in *The Big Red One*, such as the one seen here, were actually shot on location in Ireland and Israel.

Lee Marvin as Sergeant Possum, a man haunted by his actions during World War I who leads a squad of soldiers from the shores of North Africa to Germany.

Throughout the film, we occasionally see the action from the German point of view via the character of Feldwebel Schroeder – the counterpart of the US Sergeant – who is equally dedicated to his cause. Many unsettling scenes were directly inspired by Samuel Fuller's own experience of war, such as when German tanks roll over US troops screaming in their foxholes. 'When we were in those holes,' recalled Fuller, 'and the tanks were rolling over us, it was our only chance to scream all the terror out and not be heard.' The final scenes are a replay of Sergeant Possum's earlier peacetime error.

For such a gritty band of brothers movie, it has an oddly old fashioned epic quality about it. Apparently, John Wayne was originally considered for the main role. Film critic Roger Ebert neatly summed this up by calling it 'one of the most expensive B-pictures ever made, and I think that helps it fit the subject. "A" war movies are about War, but "B" war movies are about soldiers.'

GALLIPOLI

Date: **1981**   Duration: **120 min**

Director:

Peter Weir

Writer:

David Williamson

A poster for *Gallipoli*, a film about the great campaign of World War I in which Allied forces attempted to overwhelm Germany's weaker ally the Ottoman Empire. The offensive, which included troops from Australia, New Zealand, France and Britain, ended in costly failure for the Allied forces and a great victory for the Ottoman Empire.

From a place you may never have heard of a story you'll never forget.

A Peter Weir Film

GALLIPOL

ROBERT STIGWOOD · RUPERT MURDOCH FOR ASSOCIATED ''GALLIPOLI'' MEL GIBSON Executive FRANCIS O'BRIEN Screenplay DAVID W
R & R FILMS PTY LTD. PRESENT A PETER WEIR FILM   MARK LEE Producer   by

Based on PETER WEIR Produced ROBERT STIGWOOD and PATRICIA LOVELL Directed PETER WE
a Story by   by   by

Copyright © MCMLXXXI by Paramount Pictures Corporation   A PARAMOUNT PICTURE   DISTRIBUTED BY CINEMA INTERNATIONAL CORPORATION
All Rights Reserved

Mel Gibson plays Frank Dunne, a young Australian with a talent for running, who is sent to Gallipoli along with his friend Archie Hamilton (Mark Lee). This was one of Gibson's earliest movie roles and set the tone for much of his later career as he appeared in numerous other war films such as *Braveheart* and *The Patriot*.

An Australian film telling the story of Australian soldiers fighting at Gallipoli in Turkey during World War I, it shows the idealism of young men broken down by the reality of the battlefield. It stars Mel Gibson, in one of his earliest major film roles and Mark Lee, both rural workers in the Australian outback who have a talent for running. Wanting adventure and swept up by the excitement of fighting for Empire, they enlist and set sail for Egypt and then Gallipoli.

The Gallipoli campaign of 1915 was an attempt to break the stalemate on the Western Front by attacking Germany's supposed weaker ally: the Ottoman Empire. But the Turks strongly defended their position against an Allied beach landing and the campaign ended in costly failure. Mel Gibson's character, Frank Dunne, becomes a runner delivering messages for the officers in charge of an assault at the battle of the Nek and we see at first hand the poor decision-making that culminates in the loss of many lives.

The film is very much part of the Australian national mythologizing of the campaign as a prime example of Aussie soldiers misled by incompetent British commanders, historic fuel for those wishing to sever their colonial links. The year before, *Breaker Morant* had similarly questioned British imperialism and military competence during the Boer War.

In reality, the Australian soldiers at the battle of the Nek were led by Australian commanders who should bear the brunt of any criticism. The accusation that the Australian soldiers died in a diversion for British soldiers 'drinking tea on the beach' is also not true – it was a diversion for an attack by New Zealand forces. Mel Gibson went on to star in two other war films that cast the British in a poor light – *Braveheart* and *The Patriot*.

Despite the heavy-handed propagandising, *Gallipoli* is an effective piece of filmmaking and is still shown today for battlefield tours of the area. Peter Weir went on to become one of Australia's most successful film directors, directing the impressive Napoleonic naval war film *Master and Commander* in 2003. *Gallipoli* was funded by Rupert Murdoch and Robert Stigwood; Murdoch's father had been a journalist during World War I and strongly criticised the British conduct of the operation. For a campaign so much at the heart of Australian military history, it is interesting to note that more Frenchmen died in the fighting at Gallipoli than Australians.

Director Peter Weir and his production crew on the set of *Gallipoli*. Most of the filming was done in South Australia and the coastline near Port Lincoln was transformed into the beaches of the Gallipoli peninsula.

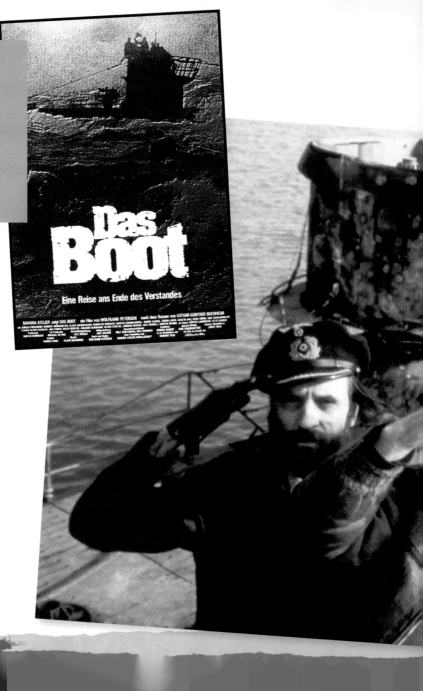

A poster for the German film *Das Boot*, an intense, claustrophobic story about the many dangers faced by German U-boat crews during World War II.

Jürgen Prochnow (centre),
Herbert Grœnemeyer (left)
and Klaus Wennemann (right)
in a still from the film *Das
Boot*.

Das Boot – 'The Boat' – is a German film set on board a U-boat as it hunts Allied shipping in the Atlantic during World War II. Despite it being the 'enemy' perspective for many Western viewers, it has become enormously popular because it communicates the awful conditions and ever-present danger faced by this submarine crew.

Based on a novel by Lothar-Gunther Buchheim, it tells the story from the point of view of a reporter sent to make a propaganda story about the crew of *U-96*. He soon finds life beneath the waves is generally tedious as they hunt for Allied ships but then, when they find one, they are bombarded by depth charges. There is tension between the new Nazi-supporting crew members and the older, more cynical veterans. In a battle with a British destroyer, they have to dive beneath its safe depth and with the craft creaking under pressure, bolts exploding and water leaking through, one of the crew panics. It is a frightening scenario, completely gripping the audience with the claustrophobic tension. When the

damaged submarine finally resurfaces, it torpedoes a ship, leaving its stricken crew to drown because they must follow orders not to take prisoners. This is 'what war is all about' says the film's German tag-line.

One of the most expensive German films ever made, the grimy detail of the submarine and its filthy crew make this an authentic tale in which the boredom and horror of the war beneath the sea is captured powerfully. An entire U-boat interior was constructed on hydraulic lifts so the vessel could be shaken to simulate depth charge attacks. Strong characterisation reveals the bonds that arise between men and the machines they work with – especially the captain, played by Jurgen Prochnow – making the final scenes appropriately moving.

Das Boot won an enthusiastic English-language audience and was nominated for six Oscars. It was later re-cut into a successful TV drama series with extra footage not used in the original movie. The original author, however, was disappointed with the final result, saying it was too melodramatic. The director Wolfgang Peterson went on to make several successful Hollywood action movies, including *In the Line of Fire*, *Air Force One*, *The Perfect Storm* and *Troy*. He was even in the running to direct the first *Harry Potter* film.

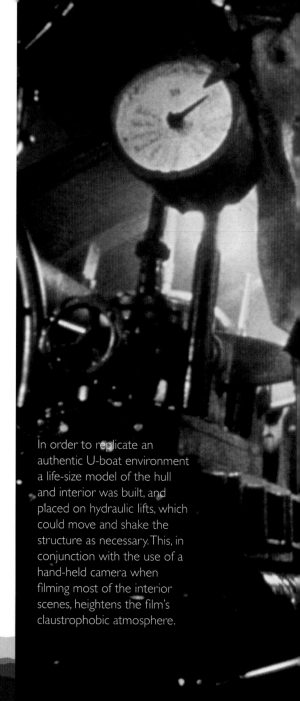

In order to replicate an authentic U-boat environment a life-size model of the hull and interior was built, and placed on hydraulic lifts, which could move and shake the structure as necessary. This, in conjunction with the use of a hand-held camera when filming most of the interior scenes, heightens the film's claustrophobic atmosphere.

Film number: **36**

COME AND SEE

Date: **1985** Duration: **142 min**

Director:

Elim Klimov

Writers:

Elim Klimov, Alexander Adamovich

A poster for *Come and See* which perfectly captures the harrowing, nightmarish vision of war portrayed in the film. The script was co-written by director Elim Klimov and Alexander Adamovich, a veteran of World War II and witness to many of the atrocities that feature in the film.

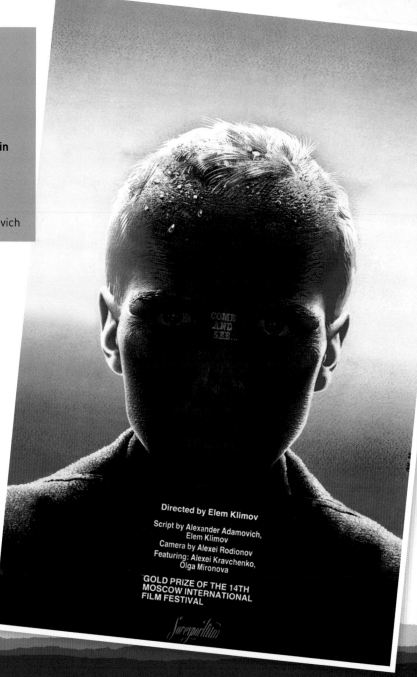

This nightmarish vision of war on the Eastern Front in World War II is a Russian film produced to commemorate the 40th anniversary of the Soviet victory over Nazi Germany. With its eerie soundtrack and child actors, it constantly seems on the edge of madness as it portrays the horrors inflicted on a village community in Belorussia by the invading Germans.

For the first part of the film, we barely see the German soldiers, their arrival from the sky more like aliens from another planet, and when the boy soldier returns to his village to see if his family are okay, he runs past the heaps of bodies piled up against a barn without even noticing them. To see the devastation of invasion through the eyes of a child is particularly effective – especially when it is a 14-year-old boy, played by the non-professional actor Aleksey Kravchenko, who desperately wants to show he is old enough to do all he can to defend his family and homeland but is clearly out of his depth facing the brutality of the Nazi war machine. A scene in which he wades through a swamp to search for his family emphasises how impossible the task is. He barely uses the rifle he proudly dug up at the start of the film. Unable to protect a village exterminated by the Germans, he is humiliated by the invaders by being made to kneel before them with a pistol against his head for a photograph –

The film's shocking and unusual approach to the brutality of war, seen through the innocent eyes of children, is particularly effective and forms a central part of the story. The lead role of Florya was played by the then 14-year-old Aleksey Kravchenko seen here (right).

an image used in posters for the film. These trophy photographs were frequently taken by German soldiers and survive as records of their atrocities.

The title comes from a line in the Bible when the reader is invited to see the destruction brought by the Four Horsemen of the Apocalypse: 'And when he had opened the fourth seal, I heard the voice of the fourth beast say, Come and see!' Nearly 30 million Soviet citizens saw the film, but, because of Cold War politics, it was not accepted as an Academy Award nominee.

The director co-wrote the film with a wartime veteran who had fought with the partisans against the Germans and experienced some of the atrocities shown in the film. The surreal quality of the film's horrors undoubtedly had an influence on Steven Spielberg when he came to direct the holocaust scenes in *Schindler's List*, and in some ways, *Come and See* is like a horrific reflection on Spielberg's earlier child/alien movies.

A scene from the 1985 film *Come and See* showing Nazi soldiers and their civilian captives. Despite the director's uncompromising approach to the upsetting reality of war the film was immensely popular in the 1980s Soviet Union.

Film number: **37**

PLATOON

Date: **1986**   Duration: **120 min**

Director:

Oliver Stone

Writer:

Oliver Stone

Academy Awards:

For best picture, director, sound mixing, and film editing

Poster for the epic war film *Platoon*. Director Oliver Stone, a veteran of the Vietnam conflict, won an Academy Award for best director, along with awards for best picture, sound mixing and film editing.

A scene from *Platoon*. In the background we can see the flames of a Vietnamese village burning wildly. The events that take place in this village are central to the film and are based on the notorious My Lai Massacre of 1968.

The first major Vietnam War film directed and written by a veteran of the conflict, *Platoon* is a semi-autobiographical account of the fighting. Oliver Stone wanted to counter more heroic versions of the war, as exemplified by John Wayne's *The Green Berets*, but Hollywood had already been proffering more cynical views of the conflict since the appearance of *The Deer Hunter* in 1978 and he initially found it difficult to attract funding for his film. An earlier version of the screenplay was sent to the singer of The Doors, Jim Morrison, to play the lead part and he was reading it in Paris when he died. The script was returned to Stone when he made a film about The Doors in 1990.

At the heart of the film is a shocking incident in a Vietnamese village. The platoon has been traumatised by seeing one of its members tortured to death and two others killed by a booby trap. As they arrive in the village to question the locals about the enemy, they are in a tense mood. One of the American soldiers, Staff Sergeant Barnes, played by Tom Berenger, shoots the village chief's wife. Sergeant Elias, played by Willem Dafoe, is furious with him and they fight, only stopping when the platoon commander orders them to leave the village. The incident is a reference to the notorious My Lai Massacre in which US soldiers slaughtered numerous unarmed Vietnamese villagers in 1968.

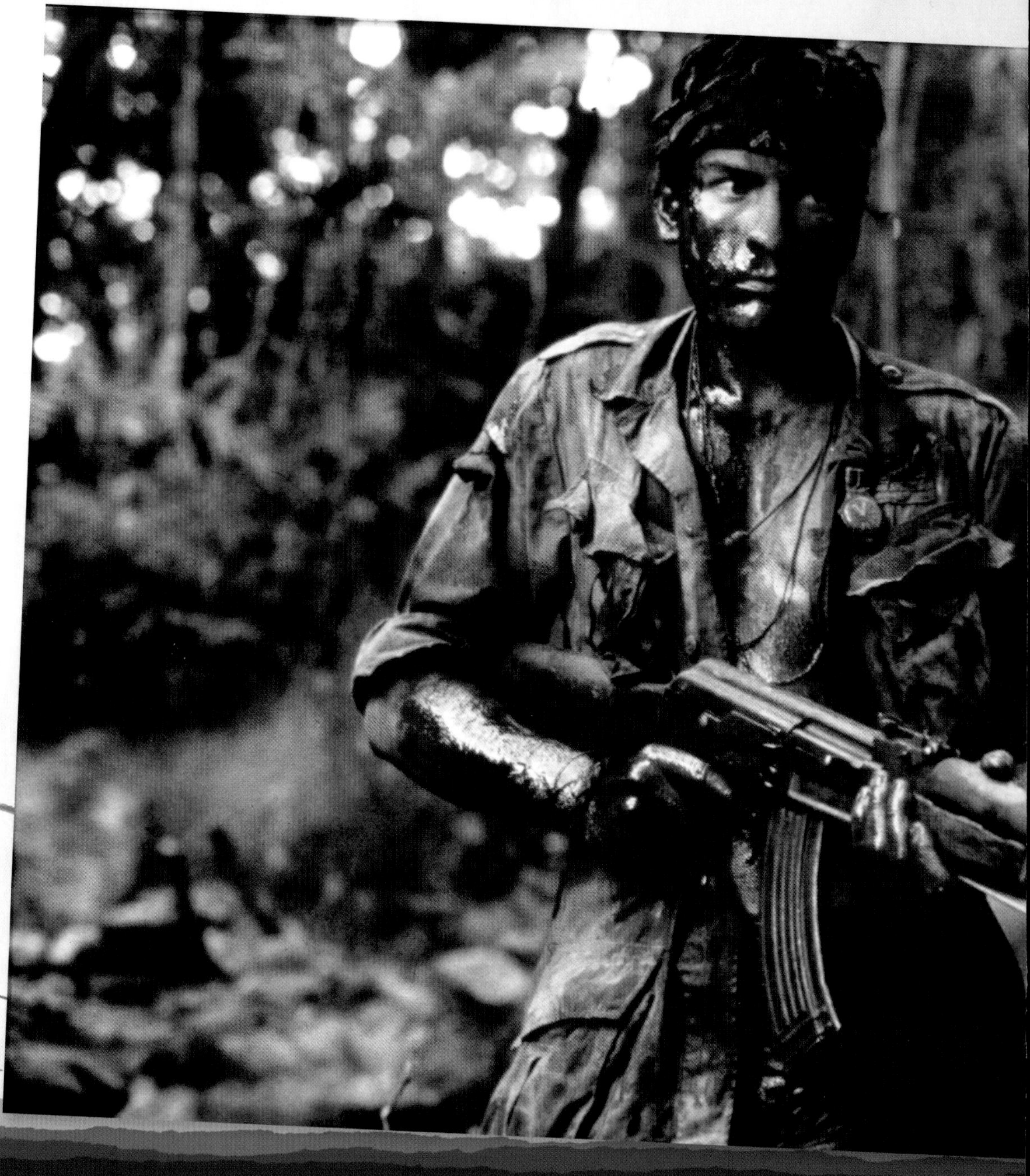

Back at base, Barnes is concerned that Elias will testify against him in a court martial and on their next patrol kills him. He lies to the rest of the platoon, saying that he was killed in action but the new recruit – the Oliver Stone figure – played by Charlie Sheen, wants to 'frag' him in retaliation. 'Fragging' was a slang term used to describe the killing of a superior officer with a fragmentation grenade so it looked as though the victim had been killed in combat.

This grim vision of an American platoon out of control, torn apart by deadly rivalry and drug taking, chimed with the anti-war spirit of the time, but now seems overly melodramatic. Nevertheless the critics were impressed with Stone's powerful filmmaking and *Platoon* won several Oscars. It became the first of a trilogy of Vietnam movies by Stone, including *Born on the Fourth of July* and *Heaven & Earth*.

Charlie Sheen as Private Chris Taylor, a college dropout who enlists in the US Army and is soon sent to Vietnam. The film's anti-war themes were very much in tune with the times, which certainly helped to bolster its popularity with both critics and the general public alike.

SCHINDLER'S LIST

Date: **1993**   Duration: **197 min**

Director:

Steven Spielberg

Writer:

Steven Zaillian

Academy Awards:

For best picture, director, adapted screenplay, original score (John Williams), film editing, cinematography (Janusz Kaminski), and art direction

The iconic poster for *Schindler's List*. The film was shot in black and white with a few exceptions, the most famous being the red coat of a little Jewish girl seen by Schindler during the liquidation of the Kraków ghetto.

The Holocaust — the attempted annihilation of the Jewish people by the Nazi regime — is such a traumatic episode in history that it seems only suited to the straight telling of a documentary and yet Spielberg manages to both communicate the horror of the experience and give us an entertaining story too. This rare achievement quite rightly received an Oscar for best picture in 1994.

Based on the novel *Schindler's Ark* by Thomas Keneally, it tells the story of the real Oskar Schindler, a German businessman who ended up saving the lives of thousands of Polish Jews. The brilliance of the story comes from the fact that Schindler is no saint, but a man looking out for himself whose self-interest also happens to preserve the lives of others. Liam Neeson is an excellent choice for the lead role as he perfectly captures Schindler's personality, most notably his ability to charm and deceive the Nazis around him.

The film is shot in Kraków, southern Poland, where Schindler actually set up his enamelware factory. To help him get on in the business community, he joins the Nazi party and wines and dines them. He recruits Jews because they are cheaper to employ. His Jewish accountant, played by Ben Kingsley, knows this will save Jews from being sent to concentration camps because it is an industry essential to the German war effort.

Ralph Fiennes plays Amon Gœth, an SS captain and commandant of the notorious Kraków-Płaszów concentration camp. Gœth was tried, convicted and executed as a war criminal in 1946, near the very site of the notorious camp.

FILM BY STEVEN SPIELBERG

CHINDLER'S LIST

When SS commander Amon Gœth – played chillingly by Ralph Fiennes – begins to eradicate the Jewish ghetto in Kraków, Schindler is shocked by the brutality. In one of the most notable scenes of the film, Spielberg communicates this by focusing on the fate of one little girl. The movie is mostly shot in black and white, but the little girl is picked out by her red coat as we watch her run away from the Nazis and hide, only to see her body later on a cart being wheeled away to be burned, still clad in her red coat.

Schindler knows he needs to remain close to Gœth and buys his support so he can employ more and more Jews in his factories. His business makes no profit as he spends all his money on Nazi bribes. The film ends in colour with real survivors – 'Schindler Jews' – paying tribute to him at his grave in Jerusalem. Despite the subject matter and because of Spielberg's story-telling skills, *Schindler's List* was an enormous commercial success.

A scene from *Schindler's List*. Behind the mounted Russian soldier we can see some of the Jewish survivors huddled together. In total Schindler saved over 1,000 Jewish men, women and children from certain death in Nazi concentration camps.

Film number: **39**

THE THIN RED LINE

Date: **1998** Duration: **170 min**

Director:

Terrence Malick

Writer:

Terrence Malick

Academy Awards:

For best picture, director, adapted screenplay, original score (John Williams), film editing, cinematography (Janusz Kaminski), and art direction

Poster for the film *The Thin Red Line* which is based on a series of fictional events that took place during the battle for Guadalcanal in the Pacific, during World War II.

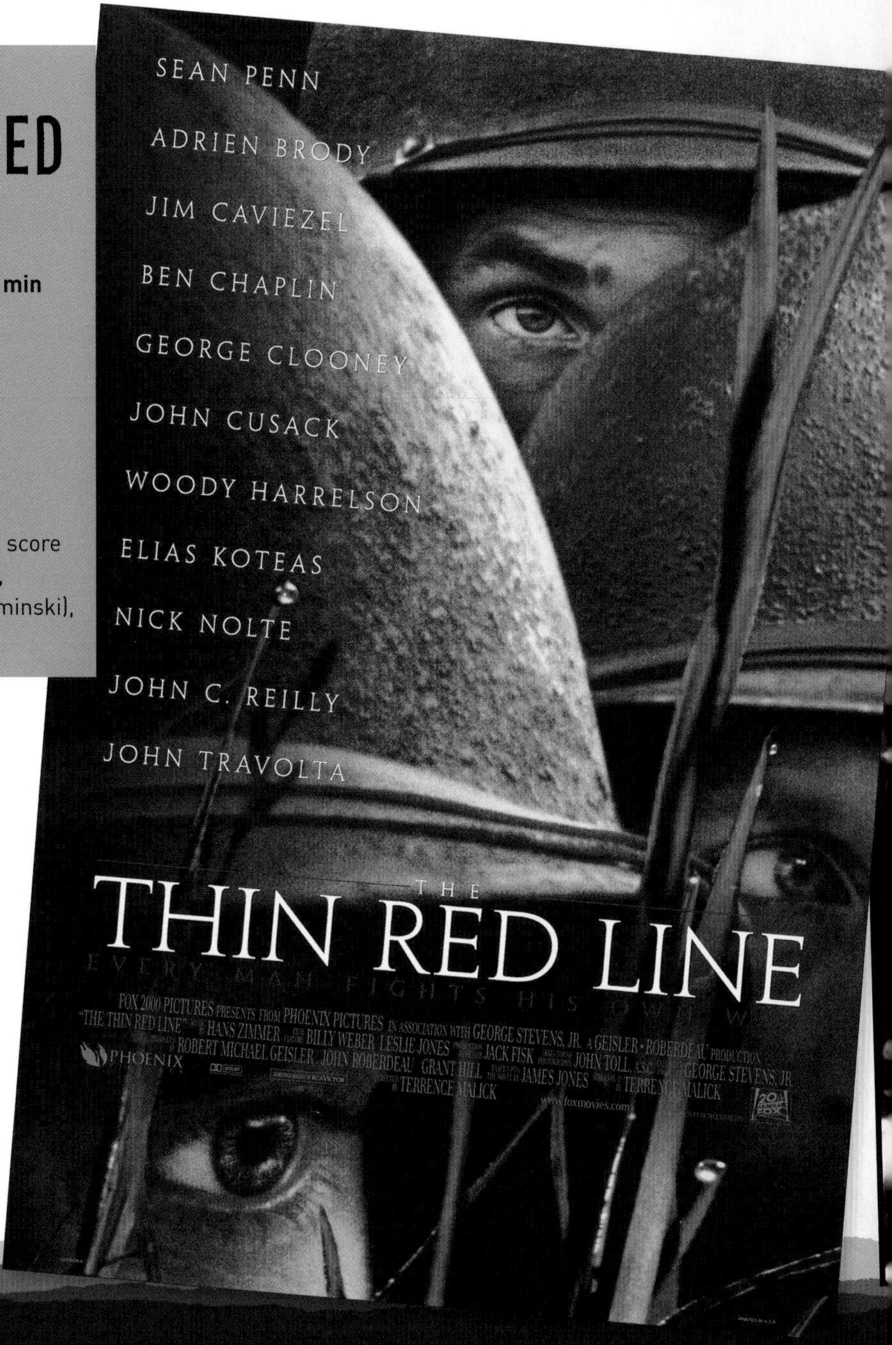

John Cusack (centre) plays a US Army captain leading a flanking attack on a Japanese position in *The Thin Red Line*.

A World War II film by the highly acclaimed Terrence Malick, the film doesn't quite match the reputation of the director. He was demanding and eccentric, and film writer Peter Biskind described him as a director 'who was very much inside his own head.'

Having made the critically praised *Badlands* and *Days of Heaven* in the 1970s, Malick then disappeared for 20 years before coming back with this war movie. The mere mention of his name attracted a stellar cast

of talented young actors, including Sean Penn, John Cusack, Woody Harrelson, Adrien Brody and George Clooney, although some later complained that their more substantial roles were cut out from the final version. It was based on the autobiographical novel by James Jones of the same name, which describes fictional action during the battle for Guadalcanal in the Pacific, and takes its title from a line in the book, not from the famous Victorian painting by Robert Gibb showing the stand of the 93rd Highlanders at the battle of Balaklava.

The film follows the lives of several young American soldiers as they arrive on the Pacific island of Guadalcanal in 1942. The set piece scene involves an assault on a Japanese bunker commanding the summit of a hill. It is the most effective part of the film as the various characters are challenged by the task of capturing the bunker – several die in surprising, random ways, giving an unsettling edge to the drama. The film explores the pressures of battlefield command and moments of sacrifice.

The juxtaposition of natural beauty with the horror of a war is a major theme that interests Malick,

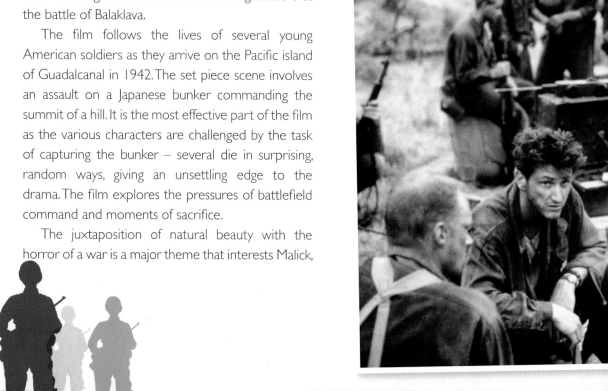

who also wrote the screenplay. In one scene, soldiers not only face Japanese bullets but a poisonous snake too. 'What's this war in the heart of nature?' says a character at the start of the film. 'Why does nature vie with itself? The land contend with the sea? Is there an avenging power in nature?' Later, one of the soldiers is intimidated by the landscape around him. 'Look at this jungle,' he says. 'Look at those vines, the way they twine around, swallowing everything. Nature's cruel.'

Critics mostly loved the movie but it failed to impress a mainstream audience, being too long and too philosophical, and it did not win any of the seven Academy Awards it was nominated for. It was filmed mostly in the rainforests of Queensland, Australia, sometimes taking up to two hours to deliver the cast and technicians to the remote locations.

Nick Nolte (centre) and Sean Penn (centre left) play US infantry in the battle for Guadalcanal in the Pacific against the Japanese in *The Thin Red Line*.

SAVING PRIVATE RYAN

Date: **1998** Duration: **169 min**

Director:

Steven Spielberg

Writer:

Robert Rodat

Academy Awards:

For best director, cinematography (Janusz Kaminski), editor (Michael Kahn), sound mixing, and sound effects editing

Publicity material for *Saving Private Ryan* emphasising that the 'mission is a man'.

The first half an hour of *Saving Private Ryan* grabs the audience with its gut-wrenching recreation of US troops landing on Omaha Beach for D-Day in June 1944. Acclaimed by many as one of the great battle scenes of all time, sound and visual effects conjure up the deadly, chaotic moments of hitting a beach in the face of enemy fire, but director Steven Spielberg said it only captured part of the reality. 'Everything you see might be over the top in graphic honesty,' he said at the time. 'But I still pull back from what I was told really happened.'

Tom Hanks (centre right) plays Captain Miller in a recreation of the D-Day Normandy landings in 1944 in Steven Spielberg's *Saving Private Ryan*.

Spielberg had been inspired to make the film when visiting the Normandy battlefields years earlier. As he walked through a war cemetery, he saw a veteran collapse to the ground, overcome by all the rows of gravestones and sobbing uncontrollably with his family around him. 'That's how this movie starts,' said Spielberg, 'It starts with something I actually observed happening right in front of me.'

The body of the film follows a squad of soldiers sent out to rescue one man – Private James Ryan – the youngest of four brothers, the other three having all been killed in action within days of each other. Captain Miller, the leader of the group, is played by Tom Hanks, Private Ryan by Matt Damon. As the soldiers press deeper into enemy territory, they question the purpose of the mission. Why is one man worth

risking eight? It is at the heart of the theme Spielberg wanted to explore. 'How do you find decency in the hell of warfare?' he questioned. 'That was the paradox that first attracted me to the project.'

The story is fictional but is based on an incident recounted in Stephen Ambrose's 1992 book, *Band of Brothers*, which was later turned into a 2001 TV drama series by Spielberg and Hanks. Ambrose was historical consultant on the film and in his book told the story of Sergeant Frederick Niland of the 101st Airborne, who was recalled from France when his mother received three telegrams on the same day telling her that her three other sons were missing in action. When Niland is finally told he can go home, he at first refuses, just as the character of Ryan does in the movie.

As Tom Hanks (left) leads his men deeper into enemy territory in *Saving Private Ryan*, they question the purpose of their mission: is one man worth risking the lives of eight others?

Film number: **41**

THREE KINGS

Date: **1999**   Duration: **114 min**

Director:

David O Russell

Writer:

David O Russell

Poster for *Three Kings*, a
satirical and sometimes dark
comedy set during the latter
stages of the first Gulf War.

George Clooney (left), Mark Wahlberg (centre) and Ice Cube (right) in the film *Three Kings*. A fourth treasure hunter, Private First Class Conrad Vig, played by Spike Jonze also joins the trio in their quest for fortune.

An amusing and sometimes surreal film set at the end of the Gulf War in 1991, it tells the fictional tale of four US soldiers wanting to make their fortune in the chaos following the Coalition invasion of Iraq. Although sold as a straightforward action heist movie, the director uses experimental art-house techniques, giving it a unique look and sound from the very start. The opening sequence shot with a hand-held camera shows one of the soldiers, played by Mark Wahlberg, wondering 'Are we shooting people or what?'

The three other fortune hunters are played by George Clooney, Spike Jonze and Ice Cube. When they discover an 'ass map' hidden by an Iraqi prisoner between his buttocks, they believe it reveals the location of gold ingots stolen from Kuwait by Saddam Hussein's army. Under cover of the ceasefire, they bluff their way into a bunker held by Iraqi soldiers to snatch the gold, but they also discover Iraqi dissidents and Clooney's character, Archie Gates, won't let his team escape with the gold without helping them.

The heart of the film arises from the Americans' desires to make a quick buck being countered by the obvious injustice around them, and their need to help others in order to help themselves. When Troy Barlow, played by Mark Wahlberg, is captured by the Iraqi army, the other three have to work with the Iraqi rebels to rescue him. In one notable scene, he is shot and we see the bullet enter his body tissue and puncture his lung, crushing his breathing. It is typical of the film's uncompromising experimental nature, combining grim authenticity with comedic scenes.

The film was shot in Arizona and California. Russell's abrasive, improvisational directing style irritated some of the filmmaking team and Clooney came to blows with him on set. 'Will I work with David ever again? Absolutely not,' said Clooney later. 'Do I think he's tremendously talented and do I think he should be nominated for Oscars? Yeah.' The film performed well at the box office and was said to be a favourite of President Clinton who had it screened to his staff at the White House. It captures a moment in time when American foreign policy believed its intervention in the troubled Middle East could have a positive impact. Two years later, *Black Hawk Down* would reveal how that could go terribly wrong.

After discovering a map hidden in the buttocks of an Iraqi soldier, George Clooney, Mark Wahlberg, Ice Cube and Spike Jonze set out to find Saddam Hussein's hidden stash of gold ingots.

BEHIND ENEMY LINES

Date: **2001** Duration: **114 min**

Director:

John Moore

Writers:

David Veloz, Zak Penn

Exciting escape drama set during the Bosnian War in the Balkans in 1995, *Behind Enemy Lines* highlights the political complexities of the conflict without losing dramatic pace. US Navy pilots played by Owen Wilson and Gabriel Macht are patrolling a demilitarised zone when they unwittingly photograph a mass grave of Bosnians killed by Serbs. The local

Owen Wilson plays US Navy Flight Officer Lieutenant Chris Burnett. Despite the film's success at the box office many critics berated director John Moore's presentation of the Bosnian conflict.

A poster for *Behind Enemy Lines*, a film about a US Navy flight officer who is shot down in Bosnian airspace and, facing certain death at the hands of a Serbian death squad, is forced to evade capture by any means necessary.

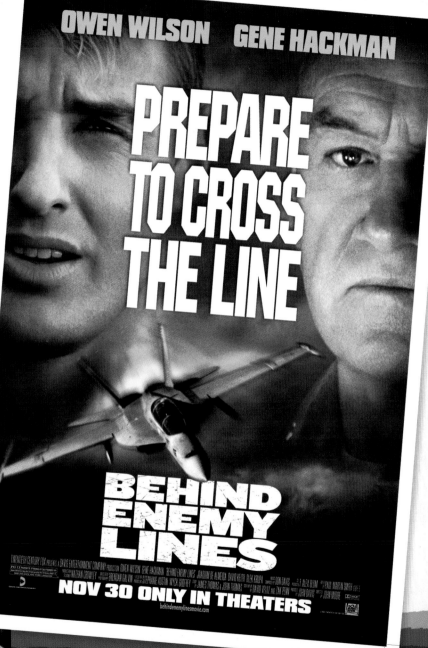

Serb warlord orders the fighter jet shot down and as the missile homes in, the two pilots eject. One of them is captured by the Serbs and executed. The character played by Owen Wilson is now forced to flee for his life across enemy territory.

The political quagmire of the Balkans is acutely revealed by the script when the surviving US pilot asks to be picked by a helicopter but is told that his presence in the demilitarised zone is embarrassing for NATO and risks jeopardising a peace accord. He must escape to a less politically sensitive location. An horrific scene follows in which he hides in the very mass grave he observed from his aircraft. Local Bosnian guerrillas take him to a nearby town that is supposed to be a safe zone but is attacked by the Serbs. Throughout the film, the reality of the situation on the ground is in stark contrast to the political machinations of his superiors. 'Everybody thinks they're gonna get a chance to punch some Nazi in the face in Normandy,' says Owen Wilson, 'but those days are over. They're long gone.' Eventually, the US Admiral has to defy NATO directives to organise a rescue mission.

The film makes good use of the unusual setting with haunting scenes and dramatic incidents. The film was shot in Slovakia and the director was nearly killed when a tank crashed through a wall while filming a scene. It has been undervalued by critics but performed well at the box office and continues to be widely screened as an exciting adventure. Moore went on to direct *A Good Day to Die Hard*.

The storyline was in part inspired by the true account of US Air Force Captain Scott O'Grady who was shot down over Bosnia in 1995 and managed to evade capture for six days before being extracted by US Marines. O'Grady was unhappy with the depiction of the main character in *Behind Enemy Lines* and sued for defamation, settling out of court with the film's producers.

Owen Wilson fights for his life as he tries to evade Serbian soldiers hunting him down in *Behind Enemy Lines*.

Film number: **43**

BLACK HAWK DOWN

Date: **2001**   Duration: **144 min**

Director:

Ridley Scott

Writer:

Ken Nolan

Academy Awards:

For best film
editing and sound mixing

A poster for the film *Black Hawk Down*. Director Ridley Scott employed an impressive array of rising young actors to play the US Delta Force operatives and soldiers of the US Army Rangers, including Josh Hartnett, Ewan McGregor, Eric Bana and Tom Hardy.

LEAVE NO MAN BEHIND

A PRODUCTION · A RIDLEY SCOTT FILM

BLACK HAWK DOWN

REVOLUTION STUDIOS AND JERRY BRUCKHEIMER FILMS PRESENT A RIDLEY SCOTT FILM A JERRY BRUCKHEIMER PRODUCTION IN ASSOCIATION WITH SCOTT FREE PRODUCTIONS STARRING JOSH HARTNETT 'BLACK HAWK DOWN' ERIC BANA EWAN McGREGOR TOM SIZEMORE WILLIAM FICHTNER AND SAM SHEPARD CASTING BONNIE TIMMERMANN MUSIC HANS ZIMMER EDITOR PIETRO SCALIA A.C.E. PRODUCTION ARTHUR MAX DIRECTOR OF PHOTOGRAPHY SLAWOMIR IDZIAK EXECUTIVE PRODUCERS SIMON WEST MIKE STENSON CHAD OMAN AND BRANKO LUSTIG BASED ON THE BOOK BY MARK BOWDEN SCREENPLAY BY KEN NOLAN AND STEVE ZAILLIAN PRODUCED BY JERRY BRUCKHEIMER AND RIDLEY SCOTT DIRECTED BY RIDLEY SCOTT

sony.com/blackhawkdown

Josh Hartnett as US Army Ranger Sergeant Matt Eversmann, leader of 'Chalk 4'. Most of the filming was done in Morocco with actors completing a short, but brutal familiarisation course with US soldiers at Fort Benning beforehand.

Based on the heart-thumping, page-turning account of a battle in Mogadishu by journalist Mark Bowden, *Black Hawk Down* explores the brutality of urban warfare through the eyes of a handful of US troops surrounded by thousands of angry Somalis. It is the Rorke's Drift of the late 20th century and Ridley Scott's brilliant film is his *Zulu*.

The humanitarian role of UN troops in Somalia was to reduce the anarchy created by warring clans. As part of this duty on 3 October 1993, 140 elite US Delta Force and Ranger soldiers made a raid into the heart of the capital city Mogadishu, to seize two key figures in the clan led by General Aidid. Using Black Hawk helicopters, it should have been a straightforward operation, quickly and effectively achieved by US troops armed with the latest weaponry. Instead, one of the helicopters is shot down and the soldiers soon find themselves in a desperate fight to extract their wounded comrades. Scott masterly ramps up the sense of dread as the small team of soldiers realise they are surrounded in the heart of the city by thousands of angry Somalis, some of them armed with automatic rifles and grenades, some just hurling sticks and stones.

For an entire night, the US troops fight a running battle with the local citizens. The firefights are shockingly and loudly recreated, and the quality of the film's picture and sound editing was rightly recognised, winning two Oscars. Eventually, the next day, the US troops manage to break out to safety, but 18 of them have been killed and 70 wounded along with over 500 Somalis killed and a thousand wounded. American firepower had proved deadly, but the benefits of advanced technology had proved moot in street-to-street fighting. The resulting loss of American lives shocked its people and quickly ended its role as world policeman.

Although documenting a military failure, *Black Hawk Down*, like *Zulu*, succeeds as a war movie because it transports the audience to the very heart of that desperate situation and shows soldiers at their best, performing professionally and looking after each other. Although light in individual character development, the sense of camaraderie is strong and makes us care about the outcome. It was a box office success and frequently features in film critics' lists of best war films. The film was shot in Morocco and the leading actors received military training from real Special Forces soldiers. At the end of their training with Rangers, some of the actors received notes asking them to 'tell our story true'. They cannot have been disappointed.

Black Hawk Down is based on the true events of October 1993 in which 140 elite US soldiers made a daring raid into the heart of Somalia's capital city Mogadishu, in an attempt to capture two high-ranking officials.

Film number: **44**

ENEMY AT THE GATES

Date: **2001**   Duration: **131 min**
Director:
Jean-Jacques Annaud
Writers:
Jean-Jacques Annaud,
Alain Godard

A poster for *Enemy at the Gates*, a film loosely based on Vassili Zaitsev, a senior sergeant of the Soviet Army and famed sniper during the battle for Stalingrad 1942–43.

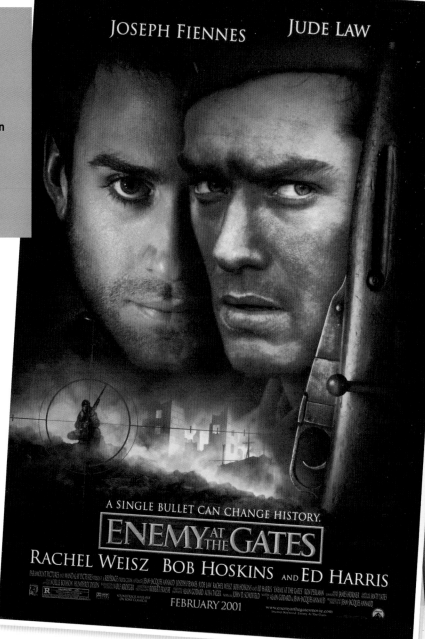

Enemy at the Gates is based on the wartime story of Vassili Zaitsev, a Soviet Russian sniper, and his exploits during the battle of Stalingrad in 1942–43. His duel with a German expert marksman fuelled local legends that grew in the telling and Zaitsev remains a national hero whose skill as a sniper is celebrated in a giant relief on the Memorial to the Battle of Stalingrad in Volgograd (the city's current name), with his sniper rifle being preserved in the city's museum.

The film starred Jude Law as Zaitsev, Ed Harris as his German sniper adversary Major Kœnig, Rachel Weisz as his Soviet soldier girlfriend, and Bob Hoskins as General Khrushchev. The screenplay cleverly explores the idea of Zaitsev's exploits being built up into Soviet propaganda to raise the morale of the city's defenders, while the exciting twists and turns of the sniper duel are purely fictional. It vividly depicts the Communist terror-machine used to frighten Russian soldiers into fighting. The love story dimension is considered to be less successful.

Director Jean-Jacques Annaud filmed it as an epic and the location for the battle scenes was a derelict factory and barracks in eastern Germany. The filmmakers

Ed Harris plays top German sniper Major Kœnig in the Stalingrad war movie *Enemy at the Gates*.

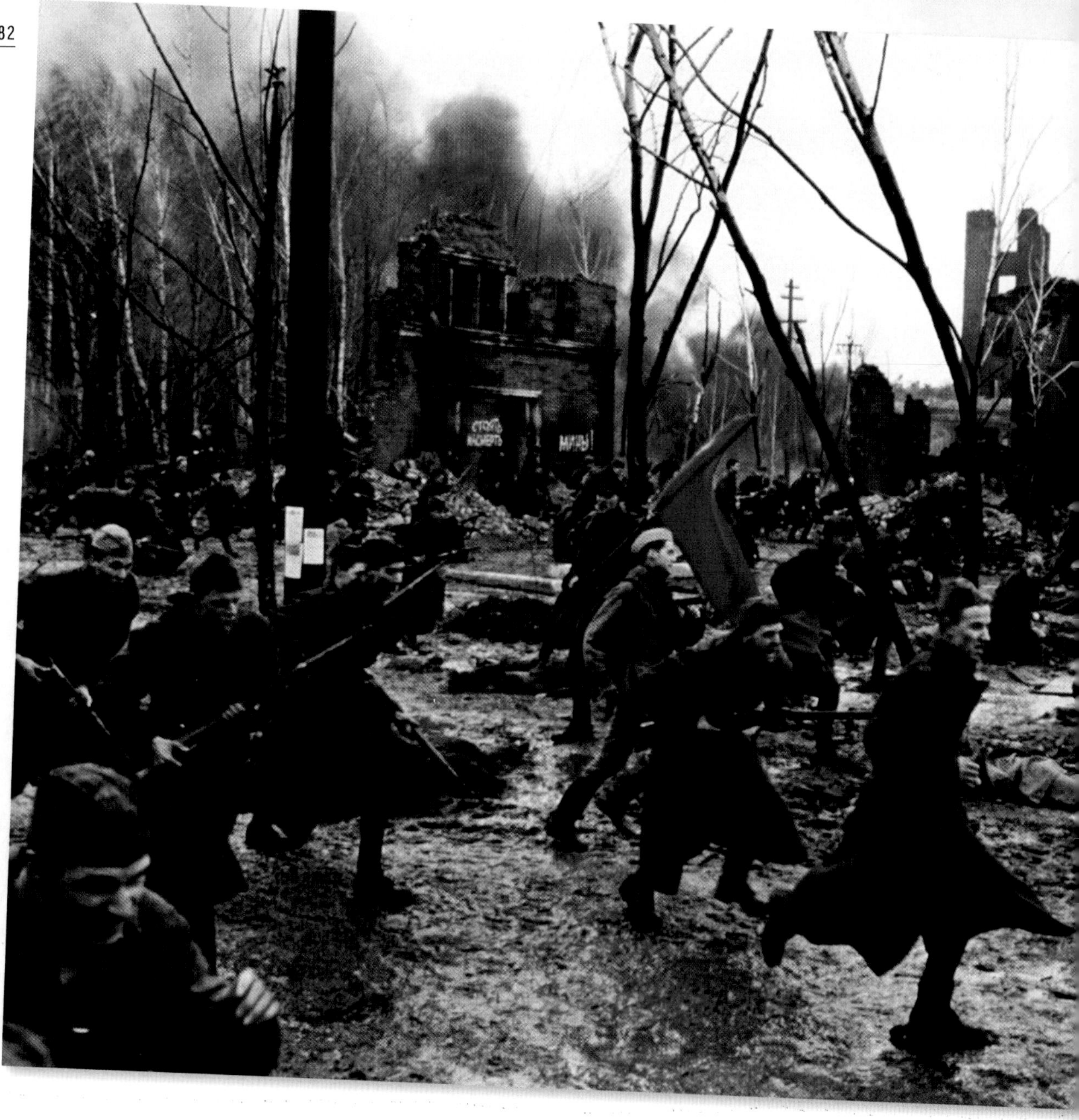
МИНЫ!

recreated the Volga River at the village of Pritzen, south of Brandenburg, where 600 extras depicted the evacuation of Stalingrad. Stunt co-ordinator Jim Dowdall trained the actors: 'All the main actors had to go through training in handling weaponry. They were trained in military fashion, starting with the basics, the loading and firing procedures until they became dexterous with their weapons. Jude Law was a fast learner, and Rachel Weisz was even faster.' Sourcing authentic looking war tanks is always a challenge for filmmakers. 'The two main German tanks we used were post-war Swiss vehicles,' said Dowdall. 'They have very updated steering gear and brakes and are beautifully manoeuvrable, and that made such a difference to us in terms of safety.'

Despite all these efforts, Russian war veterans were disappointed by the inaccuracies in the film and demanded it be banned, while German critics booed the movie at the Berlin film festival. For western viewers, it remains an unusual and dramatically exciting insight into an aspect of World War II that is rarely covered in English-language movies.

Recreated Soviet Russian assault during the battle of Stalingrad in *Enemy at the Gates*.

Film number: **45**

DOWNFALL

Date: **2004**   Duration: **155 min**

Director:

Oliver Hirschbiegel

Writer:

Bernd Eichinger

Swiss actor Bruno Ganz as Adolf Hitler in the German film *Downfall*. Ganz masterfully portrays the Nazi dictator in his final days as Soviet forces tighten their grip on Berlin.

A German film, whose original title is *Der Untergang*, *Downfall* dramatises the final days of Adolf Hitler and his Nazi regime in a bunker in Berlin as the Soviet Russian army approaches. It was notable for the star performance of Bruno Ganz as the desperate dictator raging at his subordinates.

Based on the historical writing of Joachim Fest, it captures the madness and claustrophobic atmosphere of life underground with Hitler and his closest supporters in April 1945 as Soviet shells rain down on his bunker. We see him celebrate his birthday and refusing to leave the ruined city. Having failed to persuade him to leave, SS commander Heinrich Himmler departs to negotiate peace terms with the Allies, furthering the dictator's sense of betrayal by his closest comrades.

There is no sympathy for the German civilians being killed around them and some of the most chilling scenes show die-hard Nazis executing supposed traitors to the Third Reich. 'The German people chose their fate,' says Goebbels. 'That may surprise some people. Don't fool yourself. We didn't force the German people. They gave us a mandate, and now their little throats are being cut!'

As SS troops get drunk in the bunker, Hitler orders the movement of non-existent troop units across maps of the battlefield. Much of his dialogue is based on real comments made by him and recorded by Albert Speer and his secretary Traudl Junge, who

A scene showing the evacuation of Berlin by German soldiers in the film *Downfall*. The battle of Berlin was the final major offensive by the Soviet Union and began on 12 January 1945.

features in a documentary clip at the start of the movie. We see some of the action through her eyes as a young woman working for him. 'I've got the feeling that I should be angry with this child, this young and oblivious girl,' she says, recollecting her time in the bunker, '[but] I was too curious.' The film shares that sense of curiosity when revealing the final days of the Nazi regime.

Bruno Ganz as Hitler impressed critics, with Hitler biographer Ian Kershaw saying it was the definitive performance: 'Part of this is the voice. Ganz has Hitler's voice to near perfection. It is chillingly authentic.' Other

critics feared it humanised Hitler as he wrestled with defeat, making the audience feel some sympathy for the monstrous tyrant. However, an enduring aspect of the film is that some of Hitler's scenes, where he rails in German at his demise and the failure of those around him, have been given spoof subtitles, where he instead complains about a pizza arriving late or his computer not working – all of which can be viewed on YouTube. He even rants about the existence of a website devoted to all these parodies.

A poster for *Downfall*. The film was nominated for the Academy Award for best foreign language film and received great support from critics.

Film number: 46

FLAGS OF OUR FATHERS

Date: **2006**   Duration: **131 min**

Director:

Clint Eastwood

Writers:

William Broyles Jr, Paul Haggis

Most of the epic battle scenes, including the beach landings of Iwo Jima shown here, were in fact shot in Iceland and Southern California.

Flags of Our Fathers tells the story of the six American servicemen – five Marines and a Navy man – who raised the US flag on a peak overlooking the island of Iwo Jima for an iconic photograph that symbolised victory in the Pacific War. It is based on a book written by James Bradley, the son of one of the Marines who raised the flag, which explores the lives of his father and his comrades in the war.

In the film we follow the Marines through training and watch them land on the beaches of Iwo Jima in February 1945. It is a bitter struggle against tough opposition, but eventually they raise the flag on top of Mount Suribachi. The story then reveals the true events behind the iconic image. The flag photographed by Joe Rosenthal

A poster for Clint Eastwood's 2006 film *Flags of Our Fathers*. Eastwood received a Golden Globe nomination for his role as director.

The famous scene from *Flags of Our Fathers* where US Marines of 2nd Battalion, 28th Marine Division raise the American flag atop a second peak on the Japanese occupied island of Iwo Jima.

is in fact the second one raised on the peak that day and a larger flag. Three of the men involved are then killed in the subsequent fighting on the island.

It was President Roosevelt who realised the propaganda value of the image and ordered the surviving men to return to Washington DC. They were used to raise money for the war effort in a successful war bond drive tour and the film drama takes a fascinating turn as the three men react differently to their instant celebrity. One of them, the Marine Ira Hayes, played by Adam Beach, denounces it as a farce and feels he is being discriminated against as a Native American. He drinks too much, throws up in front of a Marine general and is sent back to the fighting.

After the war, the three men are reunited for the dedication of the US Marine War Memorial sculpture featuring them, but their peacetime lives take very different paths, with Hayes still being haunted by alcoholism and feelings of guilt. Navy corpsman John Bradley only tells his story to his son on his deathbed.

The film was critically praised as one of Clint Eastwood's finest works, but was not a box office success. Although an intriguing insight into one of the war's greatest images, its depiction of war is a little self-righteous, a fault magnified in a second, accompanying film made by Eastwood, *Letters From Iwo Jima*, that tells the story of the island battle from the Japanese point of view.

THE HURT LOCKER

Date: **2008**   Duration: **161 min**

Director:

Kathryn Bigelow

Writers:

Mark Boal

Academy Awards:

For best picture, director, screenplay, sound editing, sound mixing, and film editing

A poster for *The Hurt Locker*, a film about an Iraq War Explosive Ordnance Disposal (EOD) unit. The independently made film was nominated for nine awards at the 82nd Academy Awards in 2009, winning six in total, beating rival James Cameron's critically acclaimed blockbuster epic *Avatar* for the award of Best Picture.

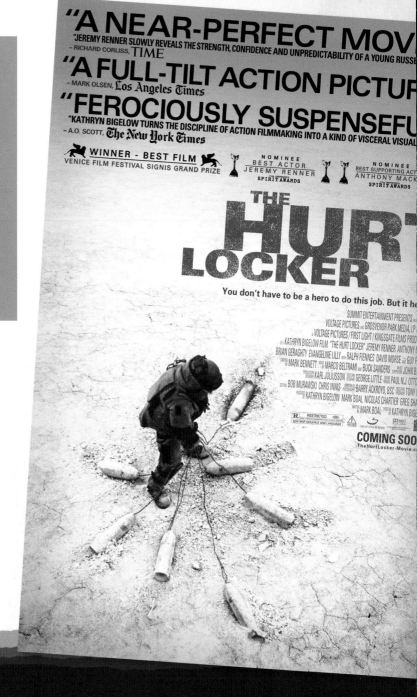

A series of bomb disposal scenarios, this film shouldn't really work as a narrative but it does as each heart-pounding incident, counting down to the end of the tour of duty, reveals another aspect of the characters and the challenges they face. Written by a freelance journalist embedded with the US Army in Iraq in 2004, it tells the story of a three-man Explosive Ordnance Disposal (EOD) team.

The film begins with a bomb disposal expert, played by leading movie actor Guy Pearce, bravely stepping up to defuse a bomb after the remote control robot breaks down. The bomb explodes and he dies. It is a shocking start as the audience really doesn't expect the director to throw away her top star in the first few minutes – a move typical of this unconventional film.

Jeremy Renner plays the replacement team leader, but it soon becomes clear that his astonishing confidence and bravery can also be reckless and a potential danger to his other team members. In an excellent scene when he briefly returns home, the usually quick-decision-making Renner cannot even decide which cereal to buy in a supermarket. He is

Actor Jeremy Renner plays Sergeant First Class William James, a battle-hardened veteran of the EOD whose reckless attitude leads to initial tension with fellow members of his unit.

only really happy when he is back on enemy soil. But the Renner character can also be kind and thoughtful to those around him and is unfailingly polite. In one horrific scene, however, his friendliness to a local child backfires, leaving him vengeful.

The film was shot in Jordan and its bleached out colouring captures the dust and heat of the region. It was made with a small budget and given a limited release to begin with but won great critical acclaim for its realism and central performance, giving it the momentum to win six Oscars, including best picture, the first for a female director. Some Iraqi veterans, however, criticised the unprofessional actions by the Renner character, saying that such a reckless figure would not normally be allowed to lead a bomb disposal team. For others, although it remains a fictional story, it gets closer to the experience of combat in Iraq than any previous movie. Bigelow went on to direct *Zero Dark Thirty* in 2012, about the hunt for terrorist Osama bin Laden.

A truly impressive piece of cinema, *The Hurt Locker* perfectly blends short scenes of intense action with a prolonged feeling of tension and suspense which lasts for the film's duration.

Film number: **48**

INGLOURIOUS BASTERDS

Date: **2009**   Duration: **152 min**

Director:

Quentin Tarantino

Writer:

Quentin Tarantino

Academy Award:

For best supporting actor (Christoph Waltz)

A poster for the film *Inglourious Basterds*. Classic 'pulp fiction' war films like *The Dirty Dozen* were a clear influence on Quentin Tarantino when he set out to create this alternative vision of World War II.

BRAD **PITT**   CHRISTOPH **WALTZ**   FA

DIANE **KRUGER**   DANIEL **BRÜHL**   SCH

INGL
BAST
THE NEW FILM BY QUENT

AN INGLORIOUS,
THRILL-RIDE OF

IN CINEMAS A

Like a war movie crossed with a 'spaghetti western', *Inglourious Basterds* also pays homage to military 'pulp fiction' classics of the 1960s such as *The Dirty Dozen*. It's an alternative vision of World War II creating completely fictional characters and scenarios set within a wartime context. This is not a film for

Eli Roth as Sergeant Donny 'The Bear Jew' Donowitz (left) and Brad Pitt as Lieutenant Aldo 'The Apache' Raine (right). Both are part of the 'Basterds', a special unit comprising Jewish-American soldiers who terrorise Nazis by killing and scalping them.

viewers wanting authenticity, but it is immensely entertaining and somehow captures the terrifyingly bizarre nature of the Nazi regime.

The film opens with Tarantino displaying his talent for building tension as SS Colonel Landa, played chillingly by the Austrian actor Christoph Waltz, searches for a Jewish family hiding beneath the floorboards of a French farmhouse. A Jewish girl, called Shosanna, escapes and vows vengeance on the

ELI
ROTH

MÉLANIE
LAURENT

Nazis. The other storyline follows a group of Jewish American soldiers, led by Lieutenant Aldo Raine, played by Brad Pitt, determined to terrorise Nazis by killing and mutilating them. They are the 'Basterds' of the title and a scene shows Hitler anxiously hearing about their exploits, including a baseball-bat wielding giant called the 'Bear Jew'.

Tarantino's obsession with the culture of movies comes to the fore when Shosanna ends up running a cinema in occupied Paris and plans her vengeance through a film premiere to be attended by top Nazis, including Hitler. More nerve-wracking scenes follow in which Shosanna is courted by a German veteran sniper starring in a propaganda film. The Basterds go under cover and there is a gloriously tense stand-off in a bar when they try to convince a suspicious Gestapo officer they are German.

The film will not be to everyone's taste but the evident absurdity of the plot allows the audience to enjoy Tarantino's taut scriptwriting and

stand-out performances by the leading actors. The mix of occasional comedy with the very real jeopardy faced by the characters – and our knowledge of the reality of the Holocaust and the Nazis – makes for unsettling but intriguing viewing that seems to be part of Tarantino's film-making technique when it comes to historical subjects. He repeats it again in his film about American slavery – *Django Unchained*. Waltz won an Oscar for his menacing role and he became a staple of Tarantino's future movies. *Inglourious Basterds* performed very well at the box office, becoming his second most commercially successful film after *Django Unchained*. The title is a reference to an Italian *Dirty Dozen*-style war movie of 1978, *Inglorious Bastards*, and plays with the idea of misspelled foreign translation titles.

A scene from *Inglourious Basterds* in which Lieutenant Archie Hicox, played by Michael Fassbender, and senior figures from the British Army, including Winston Churchill, hatch a plan to deploy the 'Basterds' to kill Hitler.

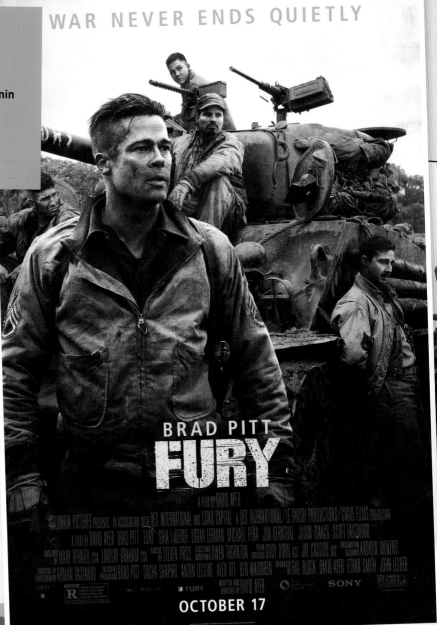

Film number: 49

FURY

Date: 2014   **Duration: 134 min**
Director:
David Ayer
Writer:
David Ayer

A poster for the film *Fury* which portrays the many horrors faced by US tank crews of the 2nd Armored Division fighting in Nazi Germany during the latter stages of World War II.

WAR NEVER ENDS QUIETLY

BRAD PITT
FURY

A FILM BY DAVID AYER

COLUMBIA PICTURES PRESENTS IN ASSOCIATION WITH QED INTERNATIONAL AND LSTAR CAPITAL A QED INTERNATIONAL/LE GRISBI PRODUCTIONS/CRAVE FILMS PRODUCTION A FILM BY DAVID AYER BRAD PITT "FURY" SHIA LaBEOUF LOGAN LERMAN MICHAEL PEÑA JON BERNTHAL JASON ISAACS SCOTT EASTWOOD CASTING MARY VERNIEU CSA LINDSAY GRAHAM CSA MUSIC STEVEN PRICE COSTUME DESIGNER OWEN THORNTON FILM EDITORS DODY DORN ACE JAY CASSIDY ACE PRODUCTION DESIGNER ANDREW MENZIES PHOTOGRAPHY ROMAN VASYANOV EXECUTIVE PRODUCERS BRAD PITT SASHA SHAPIRO ANTON LESSINE ALEX OTT BEN WAISBREN PRODUCED BY BILL BLOCK DAVID AYER ETHAN SMITH JOHN LESHER WRITTEN AND DIRECTED BY DAVID AYER

SONY   COLUMBIA PICTURES

OCTOBER 17

Director David Ayer on set
with Brad Pitt, Logan Lerman,
Shia LaBeouf, Michael Pena
and Jon Bernthal, the crew of
the M4 Sherman tank named
'Fury'.

Tanks are at the heart of this exciting movie, becoming characters in their own right as much as the leading actors. The director of several hard-hitting police movies, including *End of Watch*, David Ayer does not hold his punches when it comes to depicting life for a US tank crew on the front line of the Allied invasion of Germany in 1945.

Brad Pitt plays 'Wardaddy', the commander of an M4 Sherman tank nicknamed 'Fury' with four other crewmembers. The original driver has been killed and is replaced by the less combat experienced Ellison, played by Logan Lerman. The savage nature of the fighting at the end of the war is instantly revealed when Ellison hesitates to kill three Hitler Youth teenagers – because of their age – but they then destroy the platoon's lead tank with *panzerfaust* missile launchers. Wardaddy kills them himself and is furious at Ellison, whose hesitancy has cost them the lives of their leading tank crew. Wardaddy then pushes Ellison to execute a German soldier captured in a US uniform. There is a very tense scene in a German town when two young German women are threatened by some of the tank crew but Ellison and Wardaddy stand up to defend them – a crucial moment of shared values.

Much effort went into finding authentic, surviving tanks for the battle scenes. The last remaining, functioning Tiger I tank was located at the Bovington Tank Museum in Dorset, UK, and filmed for use in recreations of tank battles. A genuine Tiger tank had not been used in a war film since 1946.

Brad Pitt's 'Fury' Sherman tank also came from the Tank Museum, along with nine other Shermans sourced from elsewhere. The vulnerability of Sherman tanks when up against the heavily armoured and powerfully gunned German super tanks is portrayed in one edge-of-the seat scene when three Sherman tanks, one commanded by Brad Pitt, take on one Tiger. The final last-stand scenes of the movie are immensely exciting and moving.

Fury performed very well at the box office, generating a worldwide income of $212m against a budget of $68m, and gained critical praise for the director and lead actors for their efforts at authenticity. In preparation for the film, the actors endured a week-long boot camp with US Navy Seals and lived together in the tight confines of a tank.

The immensely exciting battle scene in which three M4 Sherman tanks attempt to destroy a German Tiger I. A real Tiger tank was used in this sequence, the only surviving functioning Tiger I in the world.

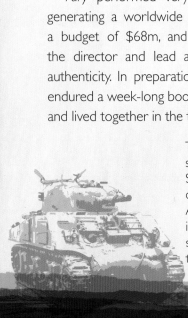

Film number: **50**

AMERICAN SNIPER

Date: **2014**   Duration: **132 min**

Director:

Clint Eastwood

Writer:

Jason Hall

Academy Award:

For best sound editing

In order to accurately portray the real US Navy SEAL Chris Kyle, Bradley Cooper (opposite) had to gain 40 pounds in weight prior to filming.

American Sniper tells the story of Chris Kyle, a top sniper for the US Navy, with 160 kills officially confirmed during his service in the Iraq War, and is based in part on his best-selling autobiography. Tragically, Kyle was killed at a firing range during the making of the film by a US veteran he was trying to help deal with battlefield trauma, an incident alluded to right at the end of the film. As with all Clint Eastwood war films, the director is at great pains not to glamorise war and the film is very much about the psychological impact it has on soldiers and their lives back home.

The film begins with Kyle being taught to shoot by his father in Texas. He enlists in 1998 and becomes a US Navy SEAL sniper. Following the 9/11 attacks on America, he is sent to Iraq in 2001 and his first kill captures the moral challenge of his task. Kyle, played by Bradley Cooper, spots an Iraqi woman give a grenade to her son and tells him to attack US soldiers with it. Kyle has to take the decision to kill the child. The mother then runs forward to pick up the grenade and continue to attack the US soldiers. Kyle has to kill her too, but is profoundly upset by it. As Kyle proves an effective sniper, the Iraqi insurgents put a bounty on his head and he becomes engaged in a sniper duel with an Olympic medal-winning shooter called Mustafa.

An Italian-language poster for the 2014 film *American Sniper* which tells the story of US Navy SEAL sniper Chris Kyle and is based in part on his best-selling autobiography.

BRADLEY
COOPER

SIENNA
MILLER

AMERICAN SNIPER
IL CECCHINO PIÙ LETALE
DELLA STORIA AMERICANA

DAL 1 GENNAIO AL CINEMA

The tense scene in which Chris Kyle must decide whether to take the life of an Iraqi child carrying a grenade in order to save the lives of nearby US soldiers.

Back home after breaks from his tours of duty, he finds it hard to balance his life as a husband and new father. Several dramatic scenes follow in Iraq in which we see the full brutality of fighting in urban settings. Kyle is now part of a team assigned with hunting down Mustafa. In the middle of a desperate firefight, he finally realises he is ready to come home and deal with his demons caused by feeling guilty about all the the comrades he couldn't help save.

The film was shot in Morocco and California. It was critically praised for its authenticity but the screenplay diverged from Kyle's own book in several ways, certainly making more of the duel with Mustafa than Kyle does himself. It was a box-office triumph, being the biggest grossing film of 2014 and Eastwood's most commercially successful war film by far.